The Truth and Reconciliation Commission

OHIO SHORT HISTORIES OF AFRICA

This series of Ohio Short Histories of Africa is meant for those who are looking for a brief but lively introduction to a wide range of topics in African history, politics, and biography, written by some of the leading experts in their fields.

The Truth and Reconciliation Commission

Mary Ingouville Burton

OHIO UNIVERSITY PRESS

ATHENS

Ohio University Press, Athens, Ohio 45701
www.ohioswallow.com

First published by Jacana Media (Pty) Ltd in 2016
10 Orange Street
Sunnyside
Auckland Park 2092
South Africa
+27 011 628 3200
www.jacana.co.za

First published in North America in 2017 by Ohio University Press
Printed in the United States of America
Ohio University Press books are printed on acid-free paper ♾ ™

ISBN: 978-0-8214-2278-6
e-ISBN: 978-0-8214-4607-2

Library of Congress Control Number: 2017947532

Contents

Introduction

It is not difficult to find reasons to criticise the Truth and Reconciliation Commission (TRC) and its outcomes, but such criticism should be based on a clear understanding of what it was established to do, and the limitations of its mandate. A commissioner myself, I came out of the TRC at the end of 1998, angry and disillusioned, mostly with myself, but also with all of us and the process itself. I felt that we had failed to live up to the grand vision that had inspired us at the outset, that we had not discovered all the truth, that we had not succeeded in drawing all those involved in the conflicts of the past into participating in the process, that we had not received nearly enough applications for amnesty from those who ought to have acknowledged their responsibility for horrendous abuses, that we had not been able to do enough for those who had suffered, and that we had not laid the foundations for the reconciliation of the huge divisions that still existed in the whole of society. We had seemed to extol forgiveness for intolerable suffering, yet only a few remarkable people had found this possible. We had offered 'the truth' to bereaved families, but had often been prevented from revealing it.

At the same time, I still believed that the commission, and the commissioners themselves, had fulfilled the necessary task of hearing and absorbing all the anger, animosity and evil which had been exposed to the TRC, serving as a form of cleansing sponge to avoid putting these back into circulation to poison the body politic. At the very least, the TRC had made it impossible for anyone to deny the atrocities which had occurred during the period it was mandated to investigate. For South Africa, the continuing responsibility should be to focus on the redemptive aspects of the commission's work, the moments of forgiveness and reconciliation, the commitment to restorative justice, the clearer understandings that had been reached, and to build on these.

Archbishop Tutu, the chairperson of the TRC, himself led the way, speaking on every possible occasion about the amazing capacity of people to forgive, encouraging others to follow, and giving other troubled parts of the world the hope that transitional justice could offer them too a way out of the past and into a better future. All of us spoke about the possibilities offered by restorative justice, rather than retribution, to allow for the rebuilding of broken and torn communities.

Yet it was already becoming clear that in South Africa there could be no reconciliation without the radical changes that needed to be faced, in order to bridge the divide that separated the privileged minority from the poor, largely unskilled majority. The long history of discrimination and exploitation would have to be reversed, if peace and justice were to be achieved.

After 1994 there were many efforts made by the new government to embark on this task, in the areas of housing, health, education and the provision of services. But it was not enough, and not fast enough, to meet the needs. Too many people remained poor and lacked opportunities to acquire education and skills. The greatly increased provision of social grants for the poorest sector has been a significant step in dealing with the inherited poverty, but on a long-term basis grants do not bring about the radical change in the redistribution of wealth that is required. Too many people have been left without trust or hope that their lives will be changed.

Disillusionment with the TRC made me feel we had done little more than facilitate the negotiated transition from the apartheid policies of the past into the newly democratic society. The promise of amnesty had indeed secured the political agreement, but we had merely scratched the surface of the gross violations of human rights that had been committed.

Eventually I came to realise that the achievements

of the TRC were not negligible. What could have been a long-drawn-out battle for power, and a destructive conflict preventing South Africans from ever coming to terms with one another, had been averted. The interim Constitution of 1993, which allowed for the end of hostilities and created the transition process, had led into the 1996 Constitution, widely recognised as one of the best in the world.

The commission's work had opened shutters into the past which could not be closed again, and further revelations would be made over the years. It was no longer possible for anyone to deny that human rights violations had indeed occurred, or to ignore the long history that had created the conditions which led to them.

There are those who consider these to be small victories, or even a betrayal. Yet other countries emerging from bitter wars look to South Africa for hope that they might achieve even some of what was secured here. Truth commissions have been part of transitional justice processes in more than 20 countries in recent years, and all have learned valuable lessons from the South African experience.

The unfinished work remains to be done: acknowledgement of the rights of the victims[1] and continuing searches for answers to their questions (such as the whereabouts of those who disappeared); prosecution of those who did not seek or receive amnesty; forms of redress that reach out to all those who were deprived of their rights under apartheid, not only those who were part of the TRC process; keeping the memories alive; drawing those who benefited and continue to derive advantages from discriminatory practices into a recognition of their responsibility to contribute to the common good.

The TRC had a specific and finite task. The remaining challenges are the ongoing task of all of us, here and now.

1

Transition

The Truth and Reconciliation Commission (TRC) emerged out of the transition to democracy which South Africa underwent in the 1990s and which was effected by a negotiated settlement between the apartheid government and the liberation movements, above all the African National Congress (ANC). It became, like the final Constitution of 1996, one of the fundamental instruments and institutions of the new constitutional and democratic order. The essential spirit that animated the TRC, if not its point of origin, was contained in the words of the Postamble to the interim Constitution, which was adopted by the negotiating parties in November 1993 and which paved the way to the first fully representative elections of April 1994. The Postamble read:

'This Constitution provides a historic bridge between

the past of a deeply divided society characterised by strife, conflict, untold suffering and injustice, and a future founded on the recognition of human rights, democracy and peaceful co-existence and development opportunities for all South Africans, irrespective of colour, race, class, belief or sex.

'The pursuit of national unity, the well-being of all South African citizens and peace require reconciliation between the people of South Africa and the reconstruction of society.

'The adoption of this Constitution lays the secure foundation for the people of South Africa to transcend the divisions and strife of the past, which generated gross violations of human rights, the transgression of humanitarian principles in violent conflicts and a legacy of hatred, fear, guilt and revenge.

'These can now be addressed on the basis that there is a need for understanding but not for vengeance, a need for reparation but not for retaliation, a need for ubuntu but not for victimisation.

'In order to advance such reconciliation and reconstruction, amnesty shall be granted in respect of acts, omissions and offences associated with political objectives and committed in the course of the conflicts of the past. To this end, Parliament under this Constitution shall adopt a law determining a firm cut-off date, which shall be a date after 8 October 1990 and before 6 December 1993, and providing for the mechanisms, criteria and procedures, including tribunals, if any, through which such amnesty shall be dealt with at any time after the law has been passed.

'With this Constitution and these commitments we, the people of South Africa, open a new chapter in the history of our country.'

The relief and exuberance that followed the 1994 elections in South Africa – those heady days that witnessed the birth of full democratic rights and led to Nelson Mandela becoming the national President – made many people wish to forget the injustices and repression of the past. Why revisit old hurts and seek to apportion blame when there was so much else the new government had to do?

More serious reflection made it clear that forgetting was not possible. The agreement reached in the final stage of the multi-party negotiations that there would be an amnesty for violations of human rights committed during the years of conflict meant that prosecution for such deeds would not be pursued. Yet it was recognised that if no account was sought for such violations, it would be difficult to build a new society founded on justice. Memories would not simply disappear, but could in fact return to undermine the progress already made and weaken the foundations of the future. Those who had suffered abuse or whose family members had been killed had a right to know the truth and to obtain some form of redress. The idealistic and far-reaching words of the Postamble kept high hopes alive over the ensuing months, as the hectic and dramatic elections took place and the new government began to put in place the necessary mechanisms to dismantle apartheid.

Among the most urgent tasks would be the need to address the inequalities arising not only from apartheid but from over a century of colonial exploitation and discrimination. Urgent requirements included access to education, land and employment opportunities, together with the provision of health services and housing, and reforms in the justice and security systems. The establishment of the Land Commission, the Human Rights Commission, the Gender Commission and the Youth Commission demonstrated the government's intentions to build a set of mechanisms to address people's rights and facilitate access to them. In addition, the new Minister of Justice, Advocate Dullah Omar, announced on 27 May 1994 that the government would establish a Truth and Reconciliation Commission, although it was over a year before the legislation providing for it was passed, in July 1995, with the promulgation of the Promotion of National Unity and Reconciliation Act. It seemed clear to many observers that these five commissions would serve as the means through which the 'reconstruction of society' and 'reconciliation' would be pursued.

Nevertheless, the decision to allow for amnesty came as a shock to many organisations working for human rights and justice, and to many people who had suffered gross violations of their rights during apartheid, or had lost family members through state-sponsored killings and disappearances or while they had been in exile. Voices were raised against the acceptance of impunity and the removal of the possibility of pursuing justice through the courts.

These deep concerns were brought to the fore by the case taken to the Constitutional Court by the Azanian People's Organisation (AZAPO), and by the Biko, Mxenge and Ribeiro families, each of whom had lost members. They argued that the provision of amnesty was a denial of the constitutional right to seek justice in the criminal courts and to bring civil actions against the state and against perpetrators in claims for compensation. They challenged the very principle of amnesty on which the commission was founded, and if they had succeeded they would have undone the entire agreement which had led to its formation.

Judgment was delivered by the Deputy President of the Constitutional Court, Mr Justice Mahomed, on 25 July 1996. The court unanimously agreed that the granting of amnesty was necessary to achieve reconciliation and that Parliament had the necessary authority to make the law providing for it. Justice Mahomed recognised the 'massive problem' of the survivors and dependants of the tortured, the killed and the wounded, but counterpoised the value of exposing the whole truth and the need to draw 'wrongdoers' into the process by offering them protection from both criminal and civil consequences. He stressed that this was not a blanket amnesty, but specifically authorised for the purposes of effecting a constructive transition towards a democratic order.

The judgment was couched in eloquent terms, recognising the legitimate resentment and grief of victims and families, but pointing to the role of the state in adopting a policy of reparations which would benefit not only specific individual cases but 'generations of children born and yet to be born', who would still suffer the consequences of poverty and deprivation generated and sustained by the institutions of apartheid.[2]

It was sobering to realise that the threat of the mainly Afrikaner right-wing to the negotiations process, and its willingness to resort to violence, had led to this compromise. In the words of Alex Boraine, later the vice-chair of the TRC, 'amnesty was the price paid for peace'.

Civil society organisations came together to consider what could be done. Many discussions were pursued in private and in the media, and two major conferences were held well before the TRC was established.[3] Examples were also considered from countries that had previously been through a similar process of transition. In particular, advice and support came from the Chilean ambassador to South Africa, José Zalaquett, who had been an opponent of military rule in his country and participated in its transition. A group led by Alex Boraine, which included members of civil society organisations and lawyers, visited Argentina to meet human rights organisations there. South Africa was fortunate in having Dullah Omar as its Minister of Justice: he strongly supported the concept of the TRC, and ensured that there was close communication between the government's legal drafting experts and those who took part in the civil society discussions.

Reluctantly accepting the provision for amnesty, the participants in these talks began to examine how it might be handled. Even if amnesty was the price for peace, amnesty itself should not come cheaply. In many of the other countries that had created some form of truth commission, amnesty had been granted in a sweeping 'blanket' form, protecting from prosecution the previous regime's security forces and those who gave them their orders. Unlike them, South Africa was not as vulnerable to a military coup, and its democratic process had been secured, and so there were more options. The tenor of the discussions was that amnesty should be applied for on an individual basis and that it should have some conditions attached to its granting, including the telling of the truth. When the legislation was drafted and came before Parliament, much of this had been incorporated. The political parties debated it at length, demanded various changes, and eventually adopted the amended version in July 1995 as the Promotion of National Unity and Reconciliation Act.

If the TRC was to succeed in its task, it would have to

be as widely trusted and accepted as possible. President Mandela appointed an advisory committee, made up of members of all the political parties then forming part of the Government of National Unity, to assist him in appointing the commissioners. They issued a call for nominations, and received 299 names. They then drew up a shortlist of 47 names and those individuals appeared in televised public interviews. From that process the advisory committee submitted 25 names to the President, and in November 1995 he made the final appointment of 17 members (the maximum number allowed by the legislation).

The chairperson was to be Archbishop Desmond Tutu, with Alex Boraine as his deputy. The commissioners were to be 'fit and proper persons who are impartial and who do not have a high political profile' (even though some of them might be known to support, or sympathise with, some political organisations or tendencies). The legislation provided that no more than two should be citizens of countries other than South Africa, but South Africa was fortunate in being able to find among its own citizens the people who could carry out this task. They represented a number of professions or occupations (lawyers, health professionals, religious leaders, civil society activists), and there were seven women among them.[4]

They met for the first time in December 1995, and were allocated to the three committees stipulated by the legislation: the Amnesty Committee, the Human Rights Violations Committee, and the Reparations and Rehabilitation Committee. By January the premises for the national office of the TRC had been obtained in Adderley Street, Cape Town, and the first full meeting took place.

The legislation provided for the co-option of up to ten additional 'committee members' to assist the Committee on Human Rights Violations, and up to five for the Committee on Reparations and Rehabilitation, with the same duties as the commissioners, and it was decided to use this opportunity to address any gaps in the composition of the commission itself. For example, it was noted that although most religious denominations were represented there was no person among them of the Jewish faith. Furthermore, there were constituencies in the population of South Africa who would still be likely to question the impartiality of the commission, and committee members were sought who might rectify this. In addition, three regional centres were established for the commission's work, in Johannesburg, Durban and East London, and the additional committee members were selected with a view to strengthening the TRC presence in those centres.[5]

Now the work could begin, in what was largely un-charted territory. The noble vision of creating a climate for reconciliation would depend on finding a measure of relief for victims, on identifying perpetrators through the amnesty process and through investigations, and on providing for a form of restorative justice. Finding ways of dealing with the past in order to allow for attention to the needs of the present was a challenge that was to be severely tested.

2

Setting up

The first meetings gave considerable attention to practical details of administration and procedures, staffing and remuneration. Commissioners were expected to work on a full-time basis, although some had prior commitments from which they first had to withdraw. They were to be remunerated on the same basis as judges, a subject which gave rise to some concern among the commissioners themselves at the large salaries and benefits this would mean. However, it was recognised that some commissioners had come from positions where they had been entitled to similar benefits, and that they all would carry a major responsibility for the outcome of the TRC.

The highest ethical standards would be required of them, and commissioners and all other members and staff of the TRC had to take an oath of confidentiality on their appointment. The administration of the oath was a regular procedure in all the regional offices as new staff members joined the team.

The chairperson stressed the absolute independence of the TRC from any political or other grouping. The commission was required by the statute to ensure that all who were considered through its work should be treated equally without discrimination of any kind. This would turn out to be the TRC's strength in the face of occasional suspicions and accusations.

It was agreed that the commission should act in as open and transparent a manner as possible, and that its relationship with the national media would be of vital importance. With this in mind it was agreed that John Allen, who had until then served as the media officer for Archbishop Tutu and who was a highly skilled and experienced practitioner, should be appointed immediately to serve the TRC in this capacity.

The way in which the media in all its forms and languages followed the work of the commission contributed to its success in reaching all sections of the population. Throughout the entire period of the TRC's existence, its work was covered by journalists, who came to know the intricacies of the process in considerable detail. John Allen's regular briefings, his proactive policy of honesty and accessibility, his willingness to handle all questions, his establishment of a team in the different regions, and his advice to members of the commission on their role in communication, all assisted in strengthening this positive relationship, even when controversial issues arose.

Other appointments made at an early stage were Hanif Vally as legal officer and Biki Minyuku as the chief executive officer, who had the responsibility for being accountable to the government for the affairs of the TRC. The university academic Charles Villa-Vicencio became the head of the research department.

An essential task at this early stage was the design and implementation of a complex information management system, with a database that would allow for the gathering and recording of a large mass of information and its subsequent analysis. Thousands of applications for amnesty, and tens of thousands of statements concerning violations of human rights, would be received and evaluated. Each of the four regional offices had to have access to the database. All of the material had to be treated with integrity and maintained with complete security. The entire bulk of the information would be used to create the TRC's Final Report.

The team that developed the database was able to draw on the experience of prior projects in other countries, such as the Haitian National Commission for Truth and Justice and the United Nations Commission on the Truth for El Salvador. They were assisted by skilled and experienced advisers and representatives of non-governmental organisations (NGOs) with a focus on human rights.

Finding the appropriate members of staff for all the different aspects of the work, and in the different regions, required skill, experience and diplomacy. Selection panels were established, but there was little time for drawing up adequate job descriptions or for long searches. Occasionally there were disagreements among the commissioners about ensuring that those appointed should include members of all South Africa's racial and ethnic groups. Eventually there were over 400 members of staff, and these had to be trained and supervised, and all had to learn to work with one another at short notice. Archbishop Tutu would remind everyone frequently to be 'kind to yourself and to those around you. If we are to seek reconciliation for the country, we must be reconciled ourselves.'

The commissioners began their work with a 'Quiet Day' in January 1996, followed by several further days of discussions. Towards the end of the marathon meeting, the chairperson insisted, 'We must get down to holding public hearings as soon as possible.' At every subsequent meeting he would stress the importance of ensuring that the voices of 'the little people' should be heard by the whole country, just as much as the well-known cases that were to be given attention.

An inter-faith 'commissioning ceremony' was held in St George's Cathedral, in Cape Town, and was attended by political party representatives, civic leaders, and many organisations and observers. Thereafter the three committees embarked on their work with a sense of urgency.

The mandate

The task of the TRC was laid down by the Promotion of National Unity and Reconciliation Act, and included the granting of amnesty, the quest for the truth about gross violations of human rights committed during the period from 1960 to 1994, and the drawing up of recommendations to the government concerning reparations and rehabilitation for the victims of such violations.

There were voices raised arguing that the commission should include in its inquiries and findings the entire spectrum of apartheid injustice: the denial of the right to vote; discrimination in the spheres of education, social services, work opportunities and housing; and, above all, the history of forced removals of individuals and communities and the ways in which the rights to the land and its mineral and agricultural wealth had largely been denied to African people.

The TRC concurred with the internationally accepted view that apartheid constituted a 'crime against humanity', and also included in this the historical context of slavery and colonialism that predated apartheid itself. The first volume of its Final Report concludes, in chapter 13, with a chronology of apartheid legislation. Yet the Promotion of National Unity and

27

Reconciliation Act made it clear that the TRC's specific mandate for the findings of 'gross violations of human rights' was to focus on what can be described as 'bodily integrity rights', such as the right to life and the freedom from torture and from cruel, inhuman or degrading treatment, from abduction and arbitrary and prolonged detention.

The Act also provided a definition of what was to be considered as a 'gross violation of human rights':

a. killing, abduction, torture or severe ill treatment;
b. any attempt, conspiracy, incitement, instigation, command or procurement to commit an act referred to in paragraph (a), which emanated from conflicts of the past and which was committed (during the mandate period) by any person acting with a political motive.

The meaning of 'victims' was also defined for the purposes of the commission as 'persons who suffered harm in the form of physical or mental injury, emotional suffering, pecuniary loss or a substantial impairment of human rights, (i) as a result of a gross violation of human rights; or (ii) as a result of an act associated with a political objective for which amnesty has been granted'. It could also include relatives or dependants of victims. These criteria provided the structure for the findings made by the Amnesty Committee and the Human Rights Violations Committee.

The period to be covered by the TRC's inquiries was

from 1 March 1960 to 6 December 1993, dates which related to the days before the Sharpeville massacre in 1960 and the enactment of the interim Constitution in 1993. This latter date was extended to 10 May 1994, in order to allow those involved in pre-election violence to apply for amnesty.

The Amnesty Committee

The Amnesty Committee was formed of two commissioners plus three other people appointed separately by the President. Of these three, one was to be the chairperson and had to be a judge, and the other the vice-chairperson, a retired judge. In fact, the President appointed three judges, Justices Hassen Mall (as chairperson), Andrew Wilson and Bernard Ngoepe, to work with commissioners Sisi Khampepe, a lawyer, and Chris de Jager, an advocate and retired politician. As the number of applications for amnesty grew, five members proved not enough, and the legislation had to be amended to provide for further appointments, up to a possible total of 19 members by 1997. Almost all the additional members were judges or lawyers, which lent the atmosphere of a court to the public hearings of amnesty applications.

The Amnesty Committee's immediate task was to draw up the official application form for amnesty, and to have it speedily promulgated and printed. Judge Mall informed the commission in January 1996 that well over 2,000 applications had already been received, but that the applicants would have to be notified that they should reapply on the official form. Eventually a total of 7,116 applications were received and registered on the database.[6]

The legislation stipulated that the Amnesty Committee 'shall grant amnesty' if satisfied that the act for which amnesty was sought was 'associated with a political objective committed in the course of the conflicts of the past' and that 'the applicant has made a full disclosure of all relevant facts'. The following criteria were outlined: a decision would be taken with reference to the motive of the person and the context of the act, the legal and factual nature of the act and its objective, and whether it had been carried out within the mandate period. It must also take into account whether the act was committed in the execution of an order, or on behalf of or with the approval of the organisation, institution, liberation movement or body to which the applicant belonged or which he or she supported. Furthermore, the decision must consider the relationship between the act and the political objective pursued (which came to be described as 'proportionality'). There was no requirement for any expression of regret or apology.

After an application had been investigated, if the committee was satisfied that these conditions had been met, it was empowered to grant amnesty to the applicant, without holding a hearing, if the act did not constitute a 'gross violation of human rights'. Similarly, after an application had been investigated, the committee was empowered to decide whether the act concerned constituted an act with a political objective. If not, it could offer the applicant the opportunity to make a further submission and, if still satisfied that there was no political objective, make a decision to refuse amnesty without holding a hearing. These decisions came to be described as those made in chambers. In both cases, the committee could inform the applicants accordingly.

If, on the other hand, these two conditions did not apply, the Amnesty Committee would follow all the necessary steps of notifying the applicant, and any person implicated, as well as any victim, of the time when a hearing would be held, and inform them of their rights to be present, and to testify and give evidence. These hearings would take place in public unless there were valid reasons to hold a closed session.

Since so many complex legal arguments were brought forward to the public amnesty hearings, they took on the nature of a judicial process, with the format of lawyers representing the applicant, any other persons implicated, and the victims or their families. In the same way as the public hearings for the victims of gross violations, they became dramatic televised events.

When a final decision was taken to grant amnesty, the commission had the responsibility to inform the applicant and, if possible, any victim. At first it was only the amnesty committee that was charged with the task of making known 'forthwith' by proclamation in the *Government Gazette* the full name of the person so amnestied, together with sufficient information to identify the act concerned. This power allocated to the committee to make the decisions concerning amnesty without reference to the full commission, and even to notify the outcomes in some cases, caused occasional confusion and misunderstandings between the separate committees. The fact that decisions were announced as soon as they were finalised gave rise to serious criticism from victims who had testified to the commission, either through statements or in public hearings, and who had waited for many months before final 'findings' were made. This provision was changed by an amendment to the legislation, promulgated at the end of November 1996, and taking effect in February 1997, to give this authority to the commission itself. In cases where amnesty was refused, the committee was bound to notify the applicant, any person who might be a victim, and the commission.

Whether amnesty was granted or refused, if the Amnesty Committee believed that any person was a victim of a gross violation of human rights arising from the act concerned, it had the task of referring the matter to the Reparations and Rehabilitation Committee for consideration.

The consequence for persons who were granted

amnesty was that they could not be held criminally or civilly liable for the act for which they had applied. If any such person had been charged with the offence, or was standing trial, or had already been convicted or sentenced, or was in custody, such proceedings or sentences would become void.

The Human Rights Violations Committee
At the start of the commission, the chairperson undertook to preside over the Human Rights Violations Committee. However, the demands on his time were so great that he was not able to fulfil that role on a regular basis, and Alex Boraine frequently acted in his place, with the lawyer Yasmin Sooka and former politician Wynand Malan as deputies. It was decided that the headquarters of the committee would be in Johannesburg.

The committee's first task was to devise a form or questionnaire, and a process for documenting the statements made by people who came forward to testify. The task was more difficult than it seemed, as there was no existing model that could be used, and the committee members had different expectations of what was to be achieved. For their part, the lawyers were conscious of the need for accurate and truthful information that could be investigated, and that would protect the witnesses as well as the commission from allegations of perjury. Others were equally concerned with the way in which the deponents would experience the telling of their story, and with devising means through which this could be part of the therapeutic and healing process. Then again, those responsible for the database reminded the committee of the need for clear facts that could be recorded in a uniform manner. Trial and error led to five versions being utilised before the final format was confirmed, making considerable additional work for the data-capturing team.

In each of the four offices, teams of 'statement takers' were appointed: their task was to listen to the accounts told to them by people who had suffered gross violations of their human rights, and to enter them onto the questionnaire. This system was intended to ensure that the essential information was recorded in English, the TRC's language of record, accurately and clearly demonstrating the details of the alleged violation. It was also intended to allow the deponent to speak in his or her own language of choice, and so all South African languages had to be provided for within the team of statement takers. Furthermore, the interview was to be structured in such a way that the deponent would feel free and safe in talking about these sensitive issues; for this reason, statement takers needed to create an appropriately comfortable atmosphere of respect and concern. For many people this might be the first time they had spoken about what they had endured, and they might take a long time to tell their story, with many extraneous details. The commission was fortunate in finding a wonderful group of people who, between them, met all the criteria to carry out this work. For the great majority of deponents, this would be the only face-to-face encounter with the TRC, and it was vital that it should contribute to their coming to terms with their past suffering.

The Investigation Unit

After the statements and applications made to both the Amnesty Committee and the Human Rights Violations Committee, the next step was the investigation process to corroborate the allegations. This was carried out by the Investigation Unit, one of the most fascinating components of the TRC, with a vital role to play. Headed by commissioner and advocate Dumisa Ntsebeza, it was made up of a mix of people – members of the previous government's security and intelligence sectors, members of the liberation movements' intelligence teams (sometimes trained in the former East Germany or the Soviet Union), journalists, human rights lawyers, and, as part of the international community's support for the TRC, international investigators with experience of similar work in other parts of the world. They brought an additional degree of impartiality and status to the team.

The Reparations and Rehabilitation Committee

A major part of the Reparations and Rehabilitation Committee's work was to draft recommendations to the government with regard to reparation to be made to those found by the commission to have indeed suffered gross violations of their human rights. The committee, which was chaired by the psychologist Hlengiwe Mkhize with Dr Wendy Orr as the deputy, embarked on a search through international agreements and examples, while at the same time giving attention to the needs and requests arising from the statements made by victims. Their proposals were discussed by the commission as a whole and formed part of the recommendations contained in the Final Report of the TRC.

The members of the committee undertook many other tasks during the work of the commission, identifying people who had special needs which could be met immediately through the provision of 'interim relief' covered by the legislation (although this took some time to become a reality). They also offered support to those who were invited to testify in public hearings, providing a team of 'briefers' who prepared the deponents for what might be an emotionally testing ordeal, and helped them through the aftermath of the hearings.

The Research Unit
This unit was created with the goal of providing informational background and context for the work of the commission. It identified periods when particular incidents had taken place, or areas where there had been a history of resistance and repression, and assisted with

the gathering of information. Charles Villa-Vicencio and his small and skilled staff contributed in a significant way to the compilation of the Final Report.

The role of the wider society
Even before the commission was actually established, there was great interest in what it might achieve, and a willingness in many quarters to assist. Organisations in civil society which had monitored and recorded human rights violations over the years, religious bodies, historians, psychologists and psychiatrists, sociologists, linguists and community activists, all made comments and suggestions, offered to make their records available, volunteered their time and expertise, and carefully observed the process.

In the Western Cape, for example, a 'Religious Response' campaign was formed as early as October 1994, arising from an initiative of the World Conference on Religion and Peace. It distributed regular newsletters and in July 1995 gave information about the selection panel for the appointment of the commissioners and its own nominations. It also outlined plans for counselling and training that it would be able to offer. In March and April 1996 it held 'forum' discussions for the benefit of its own supporters and other NGOs, and drew commissioners into meetings. It provided information about the 'Healing of Memories' workshops which were already being arranged to help deal with the traumas so many people had suffered. Other organisations too, including the Human Rights Committee, the Institute for Multi-Party Democracy, the Black Sash, the Trauma Centre for Survivors of Violence and Torture, and the Centre for the Study of Violence and Reconciliation, offered information they had gathered and volunteers to assist with TRC tasks such as taking statements or background research.

If there had been more time available, the TRC might have been able to make better use of all these offers of assistance. There was such a great sense of urgency to embark immediately on the work of gathering statements, organising public hearings and making findings, that some of the processes that might have drawn on all those offers simply did not happen. There was a view among some of the commissioners that the TRC should be able to vouch for every aspect of its work and that information gathered prior to its existence should not be considered, as the TRC would not itself be able to verify it. Some NGOs were regarded as having a particular bias, whether 'liberal' or 'progressive', which would have to be taken into account. Eventually information contributed by such organisations was used to corroborate statements made directly to the commission, and to inform the work of the research department. Historical and geographic detail could indicate areas that should be explored, or to fill in the broader context of how and where violations had taken place.

In addition to such potential help with research and practical work, there were generous offers from professionals in various fields, particularly medical and psychological, and many people gave assistance which would otherwise have been beyond the capacity of the TRC.

Meeting the President

Not long after the work had begun, arrangements were made with the office of the President for an occasion to enable President Mandela to meet the commission he had appointed. The commissioners gathered in the early morning at the Tuynhuis and waited expectantly. When the President arrived, we were dismayed to find that he did not look pleased. He then explained that he had only learned that very day that the meeting was to take place, and he would have preferred the leaders of the other political parties to be present as well. He did not regard the TRC as his own commission, but rather saw it as an independent body which should not owe allegiance to anyone. Having made his point, he warmed to the occasion, and moved generously around the room, greeting each commissioner in turn and wishing us and the whole commission well in the task that lay ahead.

3

Human rights violations and the public hearings

Chivvied along by the chairperson, the commission set the dates for its first public hearing of accounts of violations of human rights: 15–18 April 1996 in East London. Everything about the plan was designed to embody the way the TRC was seeking to fulfil its mandate, and also to highlight the significance of the Eastern Cape as an area where there had been strong resistance to apartheid, severe repression, and abuses committed both by agents of the state and by those of the liberation movements.

Led by the Reverend Bongani Finca, head of the Eastern Cape office, the statement takers spread out across the region gathering testimonies, followed by the Investigation Unit to seek verification. The difficult task of selecting those who would testify in public then began. One of the questions the statement takers were trained to ask was whether people would be willing to speak in public – it had been thought that there would be some reluctance. On the contrary, almost everyone wanted to appear, and when the selection was made, there were many angry and disappointed reactions. This seemed to confirm the value that was placed on the right to be heard and the confidence of many witnesses in the process.

The TRC had to decide how to allocate the time available in each of the hearings. Since it could not hear every one of those who had made statements, it had to find a balance that would reflect the history of each area. It sought to portray the stories of well-known events as well as those of people who had never been in the public eye; of young and old, women and men, of recent events and those that had happened decades before, and of actions carried out by agents of the security forces and also by those who supported the aims of the liberation movements. The goal was to present an overview of the violations that had taken place, leading to a wider awareness, which could prepare the way for reconciliation.

The first day opened with dramatic effect. Almost all the commissioners were present, and the people who were to testify were gathered safely away from the huge crowd. The City Hall of East London, once a symbol of white authority, was filled to capacity. Great numbers of national and international journalists, with TV cameras and recording equipment, competed for space. The stage was set with a long table for the commissioners, and a smaller table facing them, set at the same level, for the victims, each accompanied by a person to brief them. It had been decided that the commission would not occupy an elevated position on the stage – the focus was to be on those who would testify.

There had been an internal discussion as to whether the chair of the commission should wear his purple archbishop's robe. The general view was that this was not appropriate, as this was a lay commission. However, having listened to the arguments, Archbishop Tutu said gently, 'But the people will want it.' His instinct was right – his status and his history meant that people wanted to be greeted by him as they knew him, whether or not they were members of any religious faith. His robes, his blessing, and the emphasis on ritual in the public hearings – singing the national anthem or a hymn, the lighting of candles – turned out to be an important part of the process.

Everything was ready in East London, but the hearing could not begin. The police said they had received a bomb threat, and they proceeded to clear the City Hall and go through it with sniffer dogs until they were satisfied that there had been a hoax. Only then could the entire process start, with tensions heightened because of the delay.

The programme was intense and would clearly be filled with emotion. The first person to testify was Mrs Nohle Mohapi, widow of Mapetla Mohapi, who died in detention in 1976. He had been the regional organiser for the South African Students' Organisation (SASO) and a member of the Black Consciousness Movement (BCM) and the Black People's Convention. Twenty years after his death, Mrs Mohapi spoke of the importance of the BCM and the beliefs of her husband and his colleague and friend Steve Biko.

The next day brought more tragic stories, including that of the lives and deaths of the 'Cradock Four', who had been men of courage and energy in that Eastern Cape stronghold of resistance: Matthew Goniwe, Fort Calata, Sicelo Mhlauli and Sparrow Mkhonto, who had been assassinated by security forces in June 1985. Mrs Nomonde Calata rocked and wept as she relived the experience of loss and despair.

When Ernest Malgas came to speak, this long-time fighter against apartheid, arrested and detained many times, and imprisoned for 15 years, was a frail, elderly man confined in a wheelchair because of a stroke. As he described how he had been interrogated, and tortured by a method known as the 'helicopter', he broke down, while his briefer soothed him gently. This was too much for Archbishop Tutu, who laid his head down on his arms on the table in front of him and wept too. The image went instantly around the world. Later, reflecting on this experience, the Archbishop vowed he would never let himself be thus overcome again: nothing should be allowed to take attention away from the victim and the story.

Profound emotions were intensely evident as the days went on. The 33 testimonies were sometimes angry, with accusations hurled at those responsible, often described as 'the police'. All around the hall, inside as well as outside, policemen and -women were guarding the safety of the place. Many of them were young and had not lived through the years being spoken about. What would they feel as they heard these testimonies? We approached some of them to ask if they were finding it difficult, wondering whether they too would need some counselling. Some acknowledged that it was 'tough', while an older one brushed away the concern and said, 'I was just doing my job then, like I am doing it now.'

The victims who were heard came from a variety of backgrounds and political structures, and some had no particular connection with any. One was Mrs Beth Savage, who had been among a number of people severely injured or killed in an attack on the King William's Town golf club carried out by members of the Azanian People's Liberation Army (APLA), the armed wing of the Pan Africanist Congress (PAC). She brought to the hearing the remarkable example of someone able to transcend her own suffering in a quest to understand the motives of her attackers, and to offer and also to seek forgiveness.

All through these days, the radio and the television coverage reached every corner of South Africa. Although it was too much for some people to endure, it was impossible to avoid it, and the newspapers filled their pages with these portrayals of the conflicts of the past.

After the first hearing was over, the many lessons learned from it were used in preparing for all the ones still to come. There were many aspects that had to be considered in the organisation of proceedings, including the hiring and use of public halls, the provision of transport and accommodation for witnesses and staff, the security arrangements, the recording and translation equipment, and much more.

The next hearings followed rapidly all over the country: 22 April in Cape Town, 29 April in Johannesburg, three more in May, five in June, six in July, seven in August. They went on in this way until the end of the year and into the next. By May 1997 the pressure was such that eleven hearings were held that month, in Zeerust, Rustenburg, Mabopane, King William's Town, Durban, Cape Town, Piet Retief, Ermelo, Cape Town (Athlone), Balfour and Mooi River.[7]

One of the many films made about the TRC, *Red Dust,* showed a highly dramatised version of how the commission might have swept into a town in order to hold a hearing: it depicted enormous trucks, emblazoned with TRC insignia, with flags flying, driving down dusty country roads, creating huge excitement among crowds of wide-eyed children. The reality was not so colourful, but there was certainly a great deal of work entailed.

The first step was to identify an area and find a

central point from which to reach out. In the main cities this was a matter of logistics, but in more far-flung areas these decisions would be taken on the basis of information from local people, and from background knowledge provided by the TRC's Research Unit or other sources. Contact would be established with faith-based or community organisations and plans made for an initial public information meeting. This would be followed by a process of gathering statements and then making preparations for the hearings.

An account of the hearing in Beaufort West in August 1996 will serve as an illustration. This largest and oldest town of the Great Karoo, an agricultural centre dependent on sheep farming, lies on the main national road between Cape Town and Johannesburg. As it fell within the area allocated to the Cape Town office of the TRC (which handled the Western and the Northern Cape provinces), two or three commissioners and a team of staff members from Cape Town embarked on the preparations about ten weeks beforehand. The initial public meeting was arranged in a school hall in what was still regarded as a 'coloured' area, after being identified with the assistance of a local organisation. It was a little over two years since the new government had been installed, and most of the old racially defined divides remained, in a region where the population was over 70 per cent coloured, but the wealth lay in the hands of white people.

The hall was full, and the meeting had just begun when a large contingent of police vans arrived. Police personnel with sniffer dogs swept into the grounds, and announced that there had been a bomb threat: everyone must hasten outside while they inspected the premises. There was no option, and so the crowd stood outside in the cold winter evening, muttering angrily that this was simply a tactic to disrupt the event. Old hostility between the people and the police was evident, and the tension grew. One of the commissioners clambered onto an upturned rubbish bin, raised her joined hands and shouted 'Amandla', a time-honoured way of calling for calm, and then introduced familiar songs of the resistance period. Gradually everyone joined in, until the police finally emerged and allowed the meeting to proceed.

In the hall people listened to the brief explanation of the goals of the commission and the way it intended to operate in the area. After some expressions of bitter resentment about the amnesty provision, the questions poured in, about how the process would work, and how safe people would be if they offered to testify. As Mapule Ramashala responded, the audience listened attentively, clearly impressed by her strong presence. She made it clear that the objective was to seek to expose the truth about any and all violations of human rights that had taken place in the region in order to ensure that there was an accurate record of that aspect of its history, and that reconciliation between old antagonists could be pursued. The TRC could offer no incentives beyond the opportunity for people to tell of their own experiences – at that stage nothing was known about what, if any, reparations might be made available.

Much later, in the aftermath of the commission, it was alleged by some critics that people had testified in anticipation of financial reward, but we can be certain that this was not the inducement to talk. The motivation was the chance to be heard, to set the record straight, to uncover the cause of their suffering and, often, to see those responsible being called to account. The report of the Durban TRC office noted that 'the material expectations of those testifying were low. Most expressed a wish for an investigation into deaths that had occurred ... assistance with schooling ... assistance with tombstones and pensions for the elderly. At the women's hearing, counselling was requested. Very few people asked for direct financial compensation.'[8]

The preparatory meeting in Beaufort West ended with general acceptance of the process to be followed, and with practical information about where the team of statement takers would be based and the period they would remain in the town. All the statements received would be entered into the commission's records, and a limited number of witnesses from the town and the surrounding area would be asked to testify at the hearings.

Although responsibility for all the hearings lay with the Human Rights Violations Committee, the commissioners and members serving on the Reparations and Rehabilitation Committee were an integral part of the planning and execution of each of them. They shared the task of speaking at the information meetings, of finding the appropriate meeting places and of conducting the hearings, in addition to their specific role of caring for the deponents. The statements taken were part of the stream of gathering knowledge and verifying information which was the Human Rights Violations Committee's work. The Reparations and Rehabilitation Committee's work lay in the preparation of the counselling and support of the victims, in the training of the 'briefers', and in follow-up efforts to care for those most in need of assistance.

The Human Rights Violations Committee was responsible for sifting the statements received in each area, ensuring that they had been investigated and corroborated, and eventually making findings about what had happened. The first step in the verification process would be to check whether an allegation had been made against a specific, named perpetrator. If so, such a person had the right to be informed of the allegation and given an opportunity to respond. This might lead to an application for amnesty, or such an application might already have been submitted – in which case the information from the victim would be passed on to the

Amnesty Committee to be added to its investigations. On the other hand, the person so named might deny all knowledge of the case, and reserve the right to seek legal advice, which would also delay the possibility of the TRC making a finding. Sometimes there were cases of mistaken identity. I once telephoned a rural police station to speak to an official with a very common surname who had been named as responsible for ill-treatment. The young man who came to the telephone was deeply distressed: he had only recently been posted to that particular station, and he was so young that he had not even been at school when the event took place. The alleged perpetrator was never found. In a case like this, if another form of corroboration of the incident itself was found and the witness was to speak in a public hearing, he or she would be advised not to name any perpetrator.

Even if no one was named, it was essential to try to find some corroboration. Sometimes the name of a victim would be found in a police station's day book; sometimes another person had been involved in the same incident and the testimonies were sufficiently similar to serve as corroboration. The Research Unit could sometimes find newspaper articles that served to confirm the events. The Investigation Unit often discovered information to back up the statements made, but they also found that a good deal of documentary evidence had been destroyed, sometimes just before they were able to request it from a particular source.

This meant that, for many people, there was no possibility of obtaining comfort from learning more of the truth, or from seeing the perpetrator brought to book. There might be sufficient evidence to confirm a finding that the abuse had taken place and therefore to ensure that the victim would be eligible for reparations, but the truth aspect of the healing process remained elusive.

The hearing in each place, therefore, was designed in part to offer some prospect of that healing and reconciliation. In Beaufort West, after some difficulties, the hall of one of the Dutch Reformed churches was obtained for the hearing. The minister and his church council may well have had some difficulty in persuading their congregation of the wisdom of this decision. On the Sunday evening before the hearings were to begin, some of us attended the church service, demonstrating our appreciation and hoping to overcome any doubt and suspicion.

In the hall at Beaufort West when the hearing began, there were few white faces, as was common in almost all the other centres. As there was also no Archbishop to preside, the opening ceremonies were devised to build an atmosphere of respect for the stories to be heard and of hope for reconciliation and restitution.

Among the testimonies that were presented were accounts of community resistance to apartheid, and of the violence which had occurred in and around Beaufort

West. Deponents remembered incidents of brutal action by the police, and also brutal attacks on individuals who had been regarded as traitors to the liberation movements. Of particular historical interest were the memories of an elderly man who had been one of about a hundred members of Poqo, an early militia aligned to the PAC, who had been arrested and imprisoned in 1968 on charges of having conspired to poison the Victoria West water supply.

After the hearings, the TRC arranged follow-up workshops and meetings with the communities involved, as well as with individuals who might need referrals for treatment or assistance. In some cases these discussions were the start of an exploration of what reconciliation and rehabilitation might mean. The commission was conscious that it did not have the capacity to take on this task, but tried to encourage and inspire local communities to pursue it. The Reparations and Rehabilitation Committee and the briefers were sometimes able to set up structures that would continue to provide support.

The hearings based on the widespread geographical regions were mainly completed by mid-1997, and were followed by hearings with a specific theme or designed to focus on a specific event. Chapter 6 looks at the range of special hearings that were held, but here I wish to refer briefly to those that considered the experiences of young people and women.

Several hearings were designed to reflect on the

effects on youth of apartheid and of violent conflict. These were held in Durban, on 14 May 1997; Johannesburg, 12 June 1977; East London, 18 June 1997; and Cape Town, 22–24 May 1997. Witnesses who spoke at them included experts and analysts, and adults who recounted their own experiences as children. It had been decided not to invite those under 18 to testify, though many children attended the hearings, some opening the proceedings with songs or a play, others reading parts of submissions which had been tabled.

These accounts of the experiences of the youth revealed the destructive impact of apartheid on the lives of young people through the examples of those who were able to participate. Many of them had struggled to rebuild their lives after weeks, months or years of prison; they spoke of continuing physical and mental effects, of lost educational opportunities, and of young people who had died in the conflicts. These hearings had a powerful effect on the public: in some places schoolchildren attended them, gaining a glimpse of what their predecessors had lived through. The stories have inspired books and films,[9] and through these forms they continue to reverberate.

The TRC also hosted several events with a focus on the experiences of women: hearings for women only in Cape Town, Johannesburg and Durban, as well as two workshops in Gauteng. These were in part a response to approaches from organisations and academics working on gender-related issues. At an early stage in the life of the TRC, a meeting had been held in Cape Town between women of the TRC and university women to discuss the commission's approach. Despite these efforts, the experiences of women did not form such a major component of the TRC's work as might have been expected, given the number of women working in all its structures and their previous interest in gender-based rights and protections. In a society which was, and remains, strongly shaped by patriarchy, the TRC was not a feminist organisation.

Seeking to address these debates, the decision to hold hearings specifically to provide for the testimonies of women was based on several different concerns. On the one hand, many women who had made statements to the commission had spoken mainly about men – their partners, spouses, sons, lovers, fathers or brothers; they had said little about their own sufferings. Some women who had endured torture or other gross violations had experienced these in a specifically gendered form – rape, other attacks on their bodies, threats to themselves or to their children or close families, and sexual insults. Panels of women commissioners to hear their stories might make it easier for them to speak freely. These special hearings brought horrendous accounts of torture, solitary confinement, sexual abuse, electric shocks, rape and psychological torture, including threats to the women's children.

Women recounted that they had endured such violations at the hands of the security forces, or of members of opposing political organisations, and also within the liberation movements. They spoke too of the ill-treatment they had received from other women, such as female prison warders. Some of them spoke openly at the hearings, while others opted to speak from behind a screen.

The commission believed that there were many more women who had gone through such experiences, but who had chosen not to make statements to the TRC. For some of these women, what had been endured had been part of their lives in the resistance movements, and they wished neither to have those stories recorded nor to be considered in any way as 'victims'. While their right to make this choice was recognised, the hearings provided a channel through which to record that many of these stories remained untold. In spite of these efforts to listen to the stories of individuals and of particular sections of society, the commission was conscious that each hearing opened up painful histories, raised expectations of what would follow, and left behind many needs which it could not address.

The impact of all the hearings on the public was very powerful, and it was impossible for people to follow the news without being affected in some way. For some it was still denial, but for most it was a dramatic period of growing understanding of the suffering that had affected the whole country.

For the members of the commission, too, it was an intense period of work and of reflection about the events dealt with. This was particularly true of the staff members who were not in the public eye, such as the logistics teams and those who remained in the regional offices. The data capturers, for example, spent their days entering into the database the horrendous details of the statements and testimonies, the special investigations and the amnesty applications. They did not have the respite granted by travel, by encounters with fine and brave individuals, and by the actual experience of the hearings.

One of the most interesting aspects of the hearings was the process of translation. From the beginning it was clear that all South Africa's eleven official languages would have to be considered, though the mechanisms for doing this appeared daunting. Then, among the many forms of support offered by the international community, the Flemish government stepped in. 'The Flemish government?' I asked. 'There is no such thing, only the Belgian government.' However, it turned out that there is such a thing, that the Flemish section of the Belgian government does have its own structure and budgets, and has a particular interest in language rights. It provided most generously for the practical provision of the technical requirements for translation. At every hearing, glass soundproof boxes were set up, earphones were laid out on all the chairs, and instructions were given about how to operate them. At the end of each day, they were gathered up again, batteries recharged, and all were made ready for the next day.

What about the interpreters themselves? In South Africa's court system, for decade after decade, translation had been done by court interpreters, who listened first, then spoke the interpretation. There were very few who were trained or experienced in simultaneous translation. The University of the Free State offered a three-year course, but there was no time to wait for their graduates. The TRC had to find people immediately with the necessary language skills, and it was then arranged with the UFS to provide a short course to prepare them for the task.

Day after day the interpreters would sit in the hot, stuffy glass boxes, listening to graphic accounts of the suffering and violence that had characterised the years before 1994. Some of them had little political experience and little knowledge of the context of what they were to translate. Simultaneous translation requires such close attention to the words spoken, and the need to translate them quickly and accurately, that the deeper meaning of their content only follows later. Many of the interpreters found that only at the end of the day, when they were alone, or at night trying to sleep, did they feel the full impact of what they had heard and spoken. The words had gone from their ears to their mouths, in the first person: 'I was thrown into a van ... I was beaten ... I was tortured ... there was an explosion and I fell to the ground.'

After the commission had come to an end, some of the interpreters worked together with Michael Lessac, a filmmaker from the United States, to create a documentary about their experiences, called *Truth in Translation*. Since then, they have followed up this film with two more, and these have all been widely used in countries emerging from periods of conflict or repressive government.

Altogether, the TRC received some 22,000 statements about violations of human rights, and provided for the public telling of the stories of about 2,000 people. Even though the record is not complete, it provided extraordinary personal evidence of the enormous cost of apartheid, of maintaining it and of resisting it by force.

4

Amnesty

The concept of granting amnesty to persons who had committed violations of human rights was, and remains, the most controversial issue facing the TRC. It had aroused opposition before the commission was established, continued to do so throughout its existence, and has been a source of bitterness for many people ever since. International principles and conventions are generally opposed to amnesty for violations of human rights, and there are international processes established to deal with such offences. In practice, however, many countries emerging from periods of conflict or dictatorship have been obliged to consider some form of amnesty as one of the mechanisms for ensuring peace during a transition period. In such cases a new government has often been too fragile to contemplate prosecuting those who previously held power and still have the capacity to disrupt the transition. The majority of such amnesties have been granted collectively – a 'blanket amnesty', which stopped short of identifying or prosecuting individual offenders. In most cases the decisions were made through processes that were not made public.

Even in situations where criminal processes are followed, such as the Nuremberg trials in Germany after the Second World War, and the various international mechanisms in more recent times, such as the International Criminal Court and the Special Tribunals for Yugoslavia and Rwanda, prosecutions are generally brought against a few prominent individuals. These do ensure accountability for serious offences, but they do not address the large number of perpetrators who cannot be brought before these courts. They seldom give the victims of such crimes a sense of having obtained justice, nor help them come to terms with their suffering.

Finding and prosecuting perpetrators is a complex and time-consuming task. In June 2016, for example, 94-year-old Reinhold Hanning was sentenced in Germany to five years in prison for having been 'accessory to murder' in over 100,000 cases while he was a guard at Auschwitz during the Second World War, more than 70 years ago. In Argentina, after a three-year trial, 14 former military officers have recently been convicted and sentenced for their participation in Operation Condor, which was responsible for abductions, torture and killings during the 1970s and 1980s.

In South Africa, even before and then during the negotiations period, some trials were held where people were charged with torture and other violations of human rights, but where for a variety of reasons, including insufficient evidence, a conviction was not secured. The long duration of these trials, and the great expense incurred, only to end in an acquittal, did not bring satisfaction and healing to the victims. One such was the marathon trial held in 1995–6 of the former Minister of Defence, Magnus Malan, and 19 others for the massacre of 13 people at KwaMakhutha, near Durban, in 1987. Extensive evidence was led that the State Security Council had been instrumental in ensuring that the Minister provided training and support for a paramilitary unit, designed to assist the Inkatha Freedom Party in the increasingly violent conflict in the province between it and the supporters of the United Democratic Front (the UDF, which was known to support the ANC). Nevertheless, all the accused were acquitted. The matter also came before the TRC when Sergeant André Cloete applied for amnesty for his involvement in the massacre. Cloete had been a state witness in the trial. The Amnesty Committee granted him and another man amnesty, thereby indicating that it agreed that they were indeed guilty of a gross violation of human rights, and that those previously acquitted had also been so.

For the new government in South Africa after 1994, it would have been very difficult to pursue a process of bringing hundreds of perpetrators to court. Already, two Indemnity Acts, promulgated in 1990 and 1992, had allowed thousands of people to avoid prosecution. The decision to opt for amnesty was certainly also influenced by considerations of cost, and of the damage to the delicate balance of unity resulting from the negotiations, as well as the risk of violent right-wing retaliation.

The full inside story of how the decision to grant amnesty was reached has still to be told. It includes early discussions in 1992 within the ANC about a truth commission and Professor Kader Asmal's public commitment to such a process. It is also clear that the amnesty clause inserted into the Postamble to the Interim Constitution of 1993 was a mechanism to ensure the agreement which brought an end to the period of negotiations. The plan to combine the granting of amnesty, on the basis of a disclosure of the facts, with the idea of a Truth Commission seems to have come later.

Even if amnesty was the price that had to be paid for the peaceful transition to the 1994 general election and the installation of President Mandela, many people and organisations remained deeply concerned about what this might mean in terms of justice for victims of violations, and for respect for the rule of law in the new society. Furthermore, the country remained fractured in many ways. Covering up the deeds of the past and granting amnesty without investigating them would not provide a sound basis for reconciliation. Debates and discussions about amnesty, impunity and accountability gathered strength within organisations and in the media.

Meanwhile, the new Government of National Unity had other urgent tasks to address during its first year in office. It was faced with the work of rescinding the old apartheid legislation and establishing new programmes of social reconstruction. Ministries dealing with the provision of services such as health, education and housing, which had been separated along racial lines, had to be integrated and given the resources to begin to address past inequities. Provincial boundaries and systems of local government all had to be restructured. It was not until mid-1995 that Parliament could turn its attention to the question of amnesty.

Civil society organisations had for some time been considering what amnesty might mean. Two conferences brought together individuals from around South Africa, from Africa and further abroad: the first, organised by IDASA (the Institute for Democracy in South Africa), was held in Somerset West in February 1994, with a focus on 'Justice in Transition: Dealing with the Past'. Among the participants were experts on a variety of aspects of transitional justice, and also people who had suffered violations of human rights in many countries. Building on their discussions, which were published in the book *Dealing with the Past*, Alex Boraine, one of the founders of IDASA, set up a new project, Justice in Transition, which organised a second conference in July

1994, to consider a truth and reconciliation commission. The proceedings of that conference were published in 1995 in the book *The Healing of a Nation?*

Both of these events were evidence of the widespread interest in how such transitional processes might be handled in South Africa. The Open Society Foundation for South Africa offered generous support, and representatives came from many countries that had held similar commissions or other mechanisms designed to consider past abuses. They brought experience and encouragement, making it clear that the international community had a strong wish to see South Africa succeed in this project. Other discussions were held abroad, and experts in various aspects of transitional justice came forward to share their knowledge and experience. It was clear from these discussions that each country emerging from conflict and repression was constrained by the conditions under which its transition took place. Amnesties varied greatly in kind from one to another. Justice was not always possible to achieve.

In mid-1994 and well into 1995, South Africa seemed to be enjoying a period of considerable goodwill after the success of the first democratic elections. The majority of the population looked forward to great improvements in their living conditions. White people were less anxious about the future than they had been, and the climate seemed ready for reconciliation. In these circumstances it seemed possible to go beyond the granting of a blanket amnesty, and instead to require individual application and compliance with a set of criteria that would include the telling of the truth.

The new Minister of Justice, Advocate Dullah Omar, together with some of his department's legal drafters, embraced the ideas that had been discussed. Finally, the decision was reached: amnesty would be granted, but subject to conditions: self-identification of the individuals, a statement of their own version of the events concerned together with the request for amnesty, full disclosure of the circumstances and of others involved in planning or implementation, a demonstration of the political objective, and the need for proportionality between the action and the objective. Remorse or apologies were not required, but if they were forthcoming they had a powerful impact.

This was a process that might have changed the history of South Africa if it had been followed as its proponents had dreamed. If the Amnesty Committee had seen its task as part of the wider project of reconciliation and made more effort, for instance, to take into account the views of the victims; if those who had given the orders, planned the actions and rewarded the perpetrators had taken the opportunity to use the amnesty provision to reveal their roles and responsibilities; and if all of this had led to a vast improvement of the national understanding of the motives and histories of all involved, it might have altered the path of how the society evolved from there.

Each time that a previous member of the security

forces was subjected to the ordeal of a public amnesty hearing and made a full disclosure, there was the possibility of restitution for the victims concerned. When they or their families obtained a clear acknowledgement of the truth, a measure of dignity was restored to them. The mother of one of a group of young men who died at the hands of the police expressed her relief, saying, 'Now people know that our sons were not gangsters, they were freedom fighters.'

Each time that a supporter of the liberation movements, applying for amnesty, explained at such a hearing what had led him or her to commit a gross violation, this contributed to greater understanding of the conflicts of the past. The process was also aided by the fact that victims and family members were able to attend the amnesty hearings, and were assisted in obtaining legal representation. It also helped to uncover more information which the applicants might not have supplied.

Those who used the opportunity to testify fully and honestly made an important contribution to the uncovering of the truth, and to laying the foundation for reconciliation – but in the end it was not enough. Somebody at the very highest level needed to show the way. In order to set the tone for the amnesty work to succeed, those in charge who devised the policies and gave the orders – on both sides of the conflict – should have come before the TRC to seek amnesty. It seemed that the ANC sought to achieve this through its group application of 37 members for amnesty, which was submitted to the commission in 1996. This application created a major problem for the Amnesty Committee, which in fact granted a 'blanket amnesty', although it did not fit the official criteria. It was probably the intention of the ANC in thus applying to indicate its willingness to take responsibility for violations which had occurred within the ANC, even though they were unspecified. In law, however, this could not work, and the TRC itself had to appeal against this decision of its own committee, which it successfully did.

There were two other ANC group applications for amnesty in which 27 and 79 people applied, but since no specific act was disclosed by any of them, amnesty was refused. The High Command of APLA (the Azanian People's Liberation Army) also applied collectively, taking responsibility for any offences and omissions by PAC members, but since this did not comply with the requirements, amnesty was denied too.

It would seem that the spirit of these applications was consonant with the objective of the TRC, to work towards reconciliation and understanding. Given the criteria laid down by the Promotion of National Unity and Reconciliation Act, it would have been better if these indications of willingness to take responsibility had been presented at one of the special hearings for political parties. For future commissions in other countries, this is a topic that should receive consideration.

President F.W. de Klerk also made an effort to contribute to the spirit of the TRC, in the political party hearing into the role of the National Party, when he made the strongest apology ever heard before that day for the pain and suffering caused by apartheid. I was not sitting in that hearing, but I walked past a TV monitor in the passage as he spoke those words, and I rejoiced at what I saw as a major step forward. I did not know until later that the chairperson had challenged him to go further and make an apology for the gross violations of human rights committed in support of apartheid. This turned out to be too great a step to take. When the deputy chair suggested he ought to apply for amnesty, the relations between the former president and the TRC deteriorated profoundly. Max du Preez, journalist and creator of the weekly television summaries of commission hearings, has commented that this 'could have been a magical moment … [but was] wasted and it would never present itself again'.[10]

It was left to the former Minister of Law and Order, Adriaan Vlok, and the former Police Commissioner, Johan van der Merwe, to acknowledge that they had been responsible for ordering the bombing of Khotso House in Johannesburg, the building which housed the offices of the South African Council of Churches, the United Democratic Front, the Black Sash and a number of other organisations. Moreover, they stated that the instruction had come from the President, P.W. Botha. They also admitted that they were responsible for placing the blame for the bombing on an ANC activist, Shirley Gunn, who served a prison sentence as a result. Vlok also acknowledged responsibility for authorising attempts to kill the Reverend Frank Chikane, a leader within the UDF, by poisoning his clothing, and later sought him out to apologise in person.

Although the number of applications for amnesty was sometimes described as a flood, especially when the final deadline was looming, it is in fact surprising that the number was not far greater than the 7,116 who did apply. More than 22,000 testimonies from victims of gross violations of human rights were recorded by the TRC, and thousands more have claimed that they were left out of the process. This indicates that there were many more perpetrators who could have seized the opportunity to seek the amnesty offered. By doing so, they could have protected themselves against prosecution and from civil claims for damages, expunged previous convictions from their records, and contributed to the task of national reconciliation. The decision not to apply carried considerable risk and had a detrimental effect on the work of the TRC.

Why, then, did more applicants not come forward? At first it was probably a question of fear and mistrust. People waited to see how the process would work and whether the Amnesty Committee would truly be impartial. The first public Amnesty Committee hearings took place on 20 and 21 May 1996 in Phokeng, near Rustenburg. Amnesty was granted to two applicants who were serving sentences for killing the chairperson of the tribal council in the area. At the same hearing amnesty was denied to three persons who had been convicted of a killing: one of them because he denied guilt (amnesty could only be granted for an acknowledged offence), and the other two because they could not show any political motive, and because the proportionality of the act to the objective did not justify amnesty.

The public hearing of the amnesty application of the police captain Brian Mitchell, who had been convicted of the assassination of 11 people in 1988 in what came to be known as the Trust Feeds Massacre in Natal, resulted in his being granted amnesty. The six other police officers convicted in the same case had previously been given indemnity and released, while he had been given a 30-year jail sentence. Jeremy Sarkin has speculated that this decision was 'meant to act as an incentive for those liable for past crimes, to apply for amnesty'.[11]

Another reason for the failure of more perpetrators to come forward may have been a lack of knowledge and understanding of the law itself. Not everyone understood the benefit of having criminal convictions wiped off the record. Nor was there a clear grasp of the difference between the indemnities already granted (which did not provide protection against civil claims) and the amnesty offered through the TRC. The Indemnity Acts of 1990 and 1992 had given protection from prosecution to thousands of people, who therefore believed they had no need to apply for amnesty.

Some of those who had committed gross violations of human rights believed, or hoped, that their particular actions would not be discovered. There was some justification for this belief, particularly for members of the armed forces, because if no one broke rank to seek amnesty, there would be no revelations of other persons involved. Furthermore, as the criminal justice system was overburdened, as trials were lengthy, and evidence was difficult to obtain, even if they were ever tried they were unlikely to be convicted. The outcome of the Magnus Malan trial served to strengthen this belief.[12]

Even though there were few amnesty applications from leaders in the military forces, Jeremy Sarkin argues that 'the TRC process has also ensured that the involvement of the SADF [South African Defence Force] in human rights violations was exposed and recorded'.[13] Altogether 293 members of the former government's security forces applied for amnesty, including 256 from the South African Police and 31 from the Defence Force.[14]

Among those members of the military establishment who did make amnesty applications were General A.B. Joubert and Brigadier J.H. Cronje, of the SADF's Special Forces. They showed how the unit had been involved in supporting the security police in their operations against political opponents. Two anti-apartheid activists identified for elimination were Dr Fabian Ribeiro and his wife, Florence Ribeiro. Dr Ribeiro had established a medical practice in Mamelodi (Pretoria), where he witnessed and recorded the injuries of people who had been brutally treated by the police. He publicised this information abroad. He and his wife survived several attempts on their lives, but were finally shot and killed in their own home on 1 December 1986. The statements by Joubert and Cronje added to the growing body of information about state-sponsored death squads, which had first been revealed by Butana Almond Nofomela when he admitted to being part of a group that had murdered the human rights lawyer Griffiths Mxenge in November 1981. This was the spur for the eventual revelations about the notorious Vlakplaas base for such actions. Drawing on all this evidence enabled the TRC to contribute to the exposure of many secret killings, and subsequent burials, of men and women involved in trying to bring apartheid to an end.

Other amnesty requests that illustrated the role of the SADF were those of two applicants who had supplied Brigadier Wouter Basson ('Dr Death') with silencers for weapons, letter-bomb mechanisms and various items used in inflicting lethal chemicals on individuals.

The amnesty process also revealed several events of attacks carried out within South Africa by ANC operatives: the bombing of the South African Air Force offices in Church Street, Pretoria, of the SASOL oil refineries and the Voortrekkerhoogte military base in Pretoria, as well as other targets regarded as part of the apartheid establishment.

Amnesty was sought by members of APLA, the armed wing of the PAC, for the attacks on the Heidelberg Tavern and St James Church in Cape Town, on the Crazy Beat disco in Newcastle, and for the killing of the US student Amy Biehl in Cape Town, as well as other incidents. The applicants in the St James Church and the Amy Biehl attacks were already serving prison sentences after their convictions in the criminal courts. Their stories have become well known because of the contacts established with them by the families of those who were killed. In the case of Amy Biehl, the foundation established in her memory by her parents remains a testament to the process of healing they experienced and wished to share.

The strongest reason for the small number of amnesty applications and their slow submission must be the lack of clear leadership by those in positions of command. Political leaders of all parties who denied knowledge and responsibility for what had been done by their supporters, and military leaders who clamped down on information, all abandoned the lower-order perpetrators, who had believed they were obeying orders in carrying out their various actions.

Once an amnesty decision was made, there was no provision in the legislation for any appeal, except to apply to the High Court for a review. The court could either make an order referring the decision back to the Amnesty Committee for further consideration, or it could dismiss the application. By 2003 eight such applications had been filed. Two of these were successful and were referred back, three were dismissed, and three were still pending at the time of the closure of the TRC.

One of the successful applications was that of D.P. Botha, who, with A. Smuts and E. Marais, members of the Afrikaner right-wing Orde Boerevolk, had attacked a bus full of black commuters on Duffs Road, Durban, on 9 October 1990, killing seven. After their conviction in the courts, their death sentences were commuted to 30-year terms of imprisonment, and all three applied for amnesty. This was granted to Smuts and Marais, on the grounds that they were under orders from Botha, who was their superior, and that they were members of a recognised political organisation. Botha was denied amnesty since he had received no order or instructions to carry out the attack. He then brought an appeal before the then Transvaal Provincial Division,[15] which set aside the decision and made an order referring the matter back to the Amnesty Committee. The successful review did not help Botha, because, after a further hearing on 13 December 2000, the committee refused amnesty on the same basis as before, that Botha had had no authority from his organisation to launch such an attack on innocent and unarmed civilians.

The other successful review related to the killing of the 'Motherwell Four', which brought nine applications for amnesty from former members of the security forces for the murders by a car bomb of three black policemen and a black police informer on 14 December 1989 at Motherwell, Port Elizabeth. The assassination was designed to prevent possible revelations by the four men of police involvement in the 1985 killing of the 'Cradock Four'. The applicants included Gideon Nieuwoudt, who had been infamously involved in the killing of Steve Biko, and Eugene de Kock, the Vlakplaas death-squad operative who was later sentenced to 212 years' imprisonment for a whole series of murders of opponents of apartheid.

De Kock was granted amnesty for this action, since he was found to have made a full disclosure, but the Amnesty Committee refused amnesty to the eight others. Nieuwoudt, W. du Toit and M. Ras (who had been convicted and sentenced to death on 13 September 1991) contested the findings and were successful in that the High Court ordered that the decision be set aside and that, since the TRC was by that time no longer in existence, the Minister of Justice should reconvene an Amnesty Committee to hear the applications. This committee reconsidered the applications in 2004 and granted amnesty to Du Toit and Ras, but refused it to Nieuwoudt.

On 30 May 2000 the Amnesty Committee granted

amnesty to Craig Williamson and Roger Raven for the killing of the university academic and writer Ruth First, wife of Joe Slovo, in Maputo on 17 August 1982 and of Jeanette Curtis Schoon and her daughter Katryn in Angola on 28 June 1984. Both applicants were members of the security police, and the killings (by parcel bombs) were ordered, advised and planned within South Africa, even though they occurred outside its borders. Review proceedings were launched by the families of the deceased, on the grounds of the applicants' failure to make full disclosure, proportionality, personal malice, and the failure of the committee to consider all the evidence. The Cape High Court heard the matter in 2002 and refused the application.

The situation of Clive Derby-Lewis and Janusz Walus, responsible for the killing of the prominent SACP leader Chris Hani, continued to be topical right until 2016. Both applicants had been sentenced to death for the murder of Hani on 10 April 1993, but after the death penalty had been found to be unconstitutional their sentences were commuted to life imprisonment. They applied for amnesty in April 1996, and on 7 April 1999 this was refused for two main reasons: they had not proved that they had acted on behalf of or in support of the Conservative Party, although they had both been members of it; and they had not made a full disclosure of the truth in respect of various matters, including the purpose of a list of names and addresses found in

Walus's apartment, which included those of Chris Hani. They challenged the decision but a full bench of the High Court dismissed their application. They sought leave to appeal but this was denied, and when they filed a petition to the Chief Justice for leave to appeal, the petition was also refused. They were imprisoned, and over a decade later they both applied for parole, which was eventually granted to Derby-Lewis on the grounds of ill health.

When seeking to assess the value of the information gathered through the amnesty hearings, we should acknowledge that the testimonies given have enhanced our overall knowledge and understanding of gross violations of human rights under apartheid. Some victims did learn more about the circumstances of the deaths or disappearances of their family members. Some encounters between perpetrators and victims provided moments of remorse, forgiveness and healing. Most of all, the public admissions by many applicants, including white policemen and soldiers, obliged the white sector of South African society in particular to face up to the truth. They also opened the door for revelations which have continued to emerge since the end of the TRC, and no doubt will continue to do so. Some documents may have been destroyed, but others may have been secretly kept, and memories are not forgotten.

Many present-day critics of the TRC are inclined to suggest that 'thousands got off scot-free' through the amnesty process, while at the same time the victims were disregarded. This is clearly not the case, since only 1,167 amnesties were granted. But what is true is that thousands have got off scot-free because they did not apply for amnesty and have never been prosecuted. The TRC recommended that at least some of these cases should be further investigated and prosecuted, and handed over files to the National Prosecuting Authority with regard to 300 of them. However, only five cases, involving 11 perpetrators, have been prosecuted between 2001 and 2016. Several other prosecutions under way during this period were continuations of processes begun before the TRC. A few cases have finally been taken up, thanks to the persistence of survivors or their families and of human rights organisations, who have gathered considerable information themselves.

The most recent of these is the result of indefatigable efforts by the sister of Nokuthula Simelane and the lawyers who have assisted the family. Simelane, 23, was abducted, interrogated and tortured in 1983, and completely disappeared. The TRC granted amnesty to several applicants for her kidnapping and torture. Her sister, Thembisile Nkadimeng, and other members of her family continued to press for further investigations into the matter, including an inquest into her death. Nkadimeng said, 'The failure to prosecute represents a deep betrayal of those who gave their lives for the struggle for liberty and democracy in South Africa.' In February 2016 the National Prosecuting Authority

(NPA) finally announced that it would bring murder charges against four men implicated. The case will be followed with interest, since it also raises important aspects of political interference in the work of the NPA, said to be the cause of the long delay.[16] TRC commissioner Yasmin Sooka has noted that it could be a long process and the key to many other cases.

The TRC had also referred some 500 cases of disappearances to be investigated further, and in 2004 the Missing Persons Task Team was established by the National Prosecuting Authority with the responsibility of investigating such cases. It has had considerable success, and has conducted a number of exhumations, which have allowed the families of those who died to receive their loved ones' remains and to conduct burial ceremonies and arrive at a measure of closure.

Yet there has been no action in the majority of cases which could have been pursued. Not only that, but there have been attempts by the government to intervene in the process by means of the presidential authority to grant pardons, and by other proposals. President Mbeki granted pardons in 2002 to 33 people who were in prison for politically related offences, of whom 20 had been refused amnesty by the TRC. A few years later, Mbeki proposed a new pardoning process, which would establish a reference group to receive applications for pardon from people convicted of criminal offences. It would comprise representatives of the 15 national political parties, who would take into account only the perpetrators' version of the offences, denying the right of victims to participate or receive information. This plan was challenged in court by human rights organisations and survivor groups, and was found to be unconstitutional.

The National Prosecuting Authority also attempted in 2007 to find a way to deal with the backlog of prosecutions arising from the apartheid era and the revelations brought to the TRC. The plan was to grant offenders immunity according to certain criteria, which included aspects of the TRC requirements, but also added more subjective factors about remorse, restitution and other personal attitudes. Victims would have the right to argue whether charges should be dropped, but would not be able to challenge the perpetrators' stories or to have access to information derived. This was very different from the TRC process, in which victims were kept informed, and were able to be present, and to be represented by lawyers, at amnesty hearings. This plan, too, was successfully challenged through the courts.[17]

Could the TRC itself have done more to ensure justice? Perhaps if an independent post-TRC structure had been established, it might have been able to insist on prosecutions, as well as to deal with other unfulfilled commitments. Instead, it has been left to the victims themselves, and to organisations of civil society, academics and human rights lawyers (including individuals who were part of the commission) to seek further evidence, to bring pressure to bear on the National Prosecuting Authority, and to bring cases to court to seek justice.

5

Reparations

Some of the most complex aspects of the TRC's work had to do with the concept of reparation and the difficulty of translating this into reality. The issue of reparations revealed in intimately personal ways the suffering of thousands of people under apartheid, as well as the impossibility of making amends. It remains a task to be addressed on a continuous basis.

According to the legislation, the Reparations and Rehabilitation Committee was responsible for making recommendations to the President in respect of: '(1) The policy that should be followed or measures which should be taken with regard to the granting of reparation to victims or the taking of other measures aimed at rehabilitating and restoring the human and civil dignity of victims; (2) Measures that should be taken to grant urgent interim reparation to victims.' The legislation did not include any provision for the committee to undertake the actual provision of such measures, and even 'urgent interim relief' was only a subject for recommendations.

The Act defined reparation as 'any form of compensation, *ex gratia* payment, restitution, rehabilitation or recognition'. The committee's first task was to clarify for the commission what this could mean. Accordingly, the committee members undertook a study of international practice, and also entered into a national consultative process with special regard to the rights of victims. They set for themselves a definition that covered five areas: redress, restitution, rehabilitation, restoration of dignity, and reassurance of non-recurrence.

They also came to the conclusion that the question of redress, or compensation, required that one part of the reparations process should include some form of monetary grant. This raised many questions and much debate, within the commission and more widely. The very fact that those who had suffered gross violations, even death, had been denied the opportunity to pursue claims for damages (by the decision to grant amnesties) meant that they had a right to some other form of compensation. Many of them had incurred injuries which made it difficult for them to sustain themselves, or had lost family breadwinners. Many lived in abject poverty. The restoration of their human and civil dignity required financial aid and practical assistance with such services as education, health and housing.

Contrary views were also expressed. These were partly based on the difficulty of arriving at an appropriate grant, and partly on whether giving money did not somehow reduce the dignity of the survivors. 'Our people did not join the struggle to get money,' was sometimes heard, within and outside the commission, and it was true that in the public hearings not many people asked for financial help. Yet when the committee analysed the requests of those who had made statements, while often the primary wish was to know the truth, and to be told the outcome of the commission's investigations, there was also no doubt that they hoped for some help in meeting their practical needs.

It was late in 1997 when the Reparations and Rehabilitation Committee persuaded their commissioner colleagues that an individual reparation grant (IRG) should form one part of the commission's recommendations, and set about calculating how this grant might be allocated.

In the meantime, the one mechanism in place for providing some immediate financial support, defined as 'urgent interim reparation', encountered a great deal of difficulty. All commissioners, committee members and staff who came into contact with people who had made statements or appeared at hearings were aware that there were great numbers of them in urgent need of assistance, economic, physical or psychological. However, the legal framework giving the TRC the authority only to *recommend* a policy meant that the process of delivering it became long drawn out. Committee members expressed deep frustration at having to witness considerable hardship among applicants without being able to respond to it. Eventually, almost at the end of the life of the TRC, it was agreed to issue an amount of R2,000 to each of those in urgent need. By then they included a large number of the victims; what is more, some of the first people to make statements had died in the interim. All those involved agreed that the process was profoundly unsatisfactory, and that it would have been better for the TRC itself to have been granted the capacity, and a budget, for administering such funds where and when needed.

In practice, members of the Reparations and Rehabilitation Committee occasionally stepped into urgent situations by referring people in desperate need to outside agencies and NGOs for medical care, trauma counselling or other assistance. They were able, for instance, to find a wheelchair for someone whose injuries prevented him from leaving his house without assistance. They drew in expert psychiatric advice to support the application to an insurance company for a pension for someone whose injuries had caused permanent disability. The willingness of such individuals and organisations to assist was invaluable, but there was no consistent structural relationship built with them.

Having agreed on the principle of the individual

reparation grant, the committee turned its attention to the amount involved, and the mechanisms for disbursing it. The procedure followed was that the Human Rights Violations Committee would come to a conclusive finding that a person did indeed meet the criteria to be classed as a victim, and the person's name would be entered into the database, for eventual publication and for administration of the grant. Victims who were identified through the work of the Amnesty Committee could also be included through this process. The Reparations and Rehabilitation Committee would become responsible for informing these persons and supplying them with an application form for the grant. When this form was completed and returned, it would be directed to the President's Fund, which had been established to administer the payment of grants. The Fund was made up not only of the state's allocation, but of donations from various individuals and organisations.

This process had two particular implications. Firstly, people who did not wish to receive a grant would simply not apply. This outcome responded to the arguments that some victims were not in need of a grant, or that for some people it would be seen as insulting or derisory to receive money for what they had endured. Secondly, and more controversially, it meant that only people who had been found by the TRC to be victims would qualify. This led to many discussions at commission meetings. It implied a 'closed list' rather than an open one, and everyone was aware that there were many thousands of people who had not come before the commission at all, for a variety of reasons. These could include difficulty in accessing a statement taker, lack of knowledge, fear of consequences, or a negative opinion of the TRC itself. Since it had not been clear at the start of the TRC that there would be any financial benefit, this now seemed an injustice, and one that could lead to dissatisfaction and even conflict with those who had not applied or had not qualified as victims.

Eventually the difficult decision was made that the recommendation to the government had to be one to which finite numbers were attached. An open list would mean a limitless call on state funds, and would also present a major difficulty, in that there would no longer be a TRC process to carry out investigations and assess the merits of applications from victims.

On this basis, it became essential to recommend the actual figures involved. The Reparations and Rehabilitation Committee advised that the individual reparation grant (IRG) should be equally available to all victims. It could never be enough to compensate for loss of life or serious injury, and so would be no more than an acknowledgement of the harm suffered. It would be impossible to conduct means tests for so many people. Those who were wealthy or who for other reasons did not wish to apply for the grant would exclude themselves. The IRG would be made up of six annual payments of an amount between R17,029 and R23,023. The difference between the two would be calculated according to such factors as family size, and whether people were based in urban or rural areas (the latter incurring higher costs to obtain access to services). The motivation for spreading the total amount over six years was partly to ease the burden on state funds, and partly to assist families whose needs included education of children or long-term health care.

Reaching the final decisions on the policy to be recommended took a long time within the commission, mainly because the Reparations and Rehabilitation Committee explored in great detail the possible options, considered the costs, and drew in expert advice as well as the views of many of those who had made statements. At the same time, the committee developed proposals for how the other aspects of reparation could be addressed. These were to include a wide variety of community development strategies, involving the provision of health care, counselling and other services, and improvements in people's living conditions. They would also include symbolic reparations such as the naming or renaming of streets or public buildings, the building of memorials, the establishment of ceremonial events, and celebrations of history.[18]

When the TRC Report was presented to President Mandela in October 1998, and was made public, the recommendations about reparations formed one of the main topics for widespread discussion. The Report was tabled in Parliament on 25 February 1999, but no clear idea emerged about what decisions would be made by the government. Statements by some government spokespersons suggested that only symbolic and community reparations would be possible, whereas others supported at least some individual grants. Victims were left deeply dissatisfied, and were obliged to wait another four years before a final decision was taken. Only after the presentation of the final two volumes of the TRC Report was it announced by President Thabo Mbeki on 15 April 2003 that the monetary reparation grant would be a one-off amount of R30,000.

Mbeki went on to say that other reparations would consist of the construction of appropriate monuments and symbols of struggle; the systematic rehabilitation and reconstruction of communities; and the provision of medical benefits and other forms of social assistance. He also paid tribute to all those who had suffered or given their lives in the quest for liberation, and announced that the recommendations of the TRC Report would be implemented as part of the ongoing project of national reconstruction and development. The government's policy in regard to reparations was finally adopted by Parliament on 25 June 2003.

These announcements met with deeply disappointed and angry responses. TRC-defined victims had been waiting for years for the decision, they had known the content of the recommendations concerning monetary grants, and their expectations had grown. Some had become more frail and more needy during those years, some had died, some had incurred debts in expectation of the grants. In addition, thousands more people who believed they could have qualified in the same way for reparations if they had made statements to the TRC, had been campaigning to be included, but now found themselves definitely excluded. The other recommendations about broader forms of reparations faded into the background in the face of their angry reactions.

Some of this resentment could have been averted if the government had discussed the Report when it was first tabled in Parliament. The decision to adopt a smaller financial grant might have been accepted then, especially if it had been accompanied by assurances of the intention to embark on 'community reparations' which would benefit all citizens. But the long delay made many people feel unacknowledged and unappreciated.

During the months after the presentation of the Report in October 1998, when only the Amnesty Committee remained officially in place, a small team worked on completing the findings process by notifying the victims of gross violations that they were entitled to apply for reparations and sending them the necessary forms. The President's Fund had been established, and after 2003 began to transfer the agreed grant to those whose applications were received and processed. Difficulties still arose when it was found that some victims had died, some had moved away from their place of residence without leaving a change of address, or were otherwise difficult to trace. By June 2005 about 1,700 people remained to be paid their grant.

The Khulumani Support Group, which represents survivors of gross human rights violations who did not come before the TRC, maintains a database of more than 90,000 people who argue that they meet the criteria of its definition of victims – killings, abductions, torture and severe ill-treatment (known as KATS). The government, however, has not changed its policy of allocating grants only to those identified through the TRC process.

A considerable sum remains in the President's Fund – in 2016 it was said to stand at R1 billion. Over the years there have been suggestions of transferring it to, for example, the Road Accident Fund or other emergency funds, though this evoked strong opposition – not only from victims, but from donors too, who could be justly critical if the funds they contributed were used for a different purpose. The difficulty lies in identifying projects which meet the objectives outlined in the TRC's recommendations. Assistance with health or educational needs would require some form of assessment, and would have to be managed in ways that do not advantage certain people over others.

Some of the symbolic reparations programmes have

been promoted by different government departments, both national and provincial, such as the naming of streets or buildings or areas in memory of those who died in the struggle against apartheid. Others have taken the form of building or recreating museums or memorial sites, such as Freedom Park, Walter Sisulu Square and the Hector Pieterson Museum. Not all of these projects have specifically defined themselves as responding to the TRC's proposals, but they do point to the need to continue learning from our past history in order to work towards reconciliation.

A number of healing ceremonies were designed by various faith-based organisations, and carried out in different areas; and programmes such as the 'Healing of Memories' continue to work with people who suffer trauma from what they endured. These workshops, originally conceived by the Reverend Michael Lapsley, himself severely injured by a letter bomb sent by agents of the security forces, were conducted first in Cape Town and then in other cities and countries, and have helped thousands of people to find ways of dealing with their experiences and loss.

One of the aspects of reparations which remain to be developed is that of community reparations. The Department of Justice has put forward plans for awarding grants to two 'communities' in each province, for projects which such communities themselves will identify, according to certain criteria, principally related to creating infrastructure for development. It is not clear how widely the Department has consulted with organisations and individuals in the communities identified. More complex is the question of facilitating access for survivors and their dependants to specific services such as educational or health needs. This would require a process of assessment and identification.

To monitor progress on these issues of reparations, as well as to keep a watching brief on the unfinished work of prosecutions or the possibility of pardons, the South African Coalition for Transitional Justice brings together a number of organisations.[19] It continues to explore the possibility of reopening the list of victims, and to press for a transparent and comprehensive process of consultation with local communities and organisations about the community reparations process.

The whole question of reparations is the subject of an ongoing debate within the field of transitional justice. Pablo de Greiff, who is a recognised world authority on the subject, argues that justice requires some measure of compensation for those who suffered violations of human rights, while at the same time a way must be sought of designing an appropriate means of reparation in mass cases. He stresses the importance of providing recognition to victims, as well as ensuring their participation.[20] Yet the reality is that in many countries emerging from devastating wars or conflict, the economic situation is so desperate that there is simply no possibility of making financial reparations. The best that can be hoped for is the promise of peace and security, and an assurance of non-repetition of abuse.

In countries where financial reparations are possible, they should form part of the process of reconciliation and justice. The Truth and Reconciliation Commission of Canada, for example, has been dealing with reparations for the ill-treatment of indigenous people, particularly children taken into residential schools and deprived of their cultural heritage. It has recommended financial compensation, and an adjudication process is currently underway to implement this.

In order to avoid the difficulties that were experienced in seeking to implement the recommendations of the South African commission, and in taking them further, other countries embarking on similar undertakings might consider including in the original planning and legislation a mechanism or an ongoing structure to pursue and implement its recommendations.

6

Special hearings

'It is almost impossible to understand how, over the years, people ... found themselves turning a blind eye to a system which impoverished, oppressed and violated the lives and very existence of so many of their fellow citizens ... What is clear is that apartheid could only have happened if large numbers of enfranchised, relatively privileged South Africans either condoned or simply allowed it to continue. How did so many people, working within so many influential sectors and institutions, react to what was happening around them? Did they know it was happening? If they did not know, or did not believe it was happening, from where did they derive their ignorance or their misunderstanding?'[21]

With these words, the TRC Report introduced the chapter on the institutional and special hearings. Through these inquiries, the commission sought to deepen its understanding of how various sectors of society had functioned during the years of political conflict and even before. Had they willingly or unwillingly contributed to sustaining the status quo? Had they enabled the development of opposition or resistance and begun to contemplate a future beyond discrimination and separation? Had they tried to uphold international standards of human rights and protections?

In the search for answers, the commission decided to invite all the political parties to attend hearings and to make submissions and answer questions about their policies. It also organised public hearings to focus on different aspects of the country's institutions and on specific major themes.

The political parties

The TRC called on the political parties to make written and public submissions covering their policies and practices during the years of its mandate. After many negotiations, the date was set for a public hearing over four days in August 1996. Wendy Orr recalls that the order of presentation was decided by drawing numbers out of a hat, to ensure fair play. The Freedom Front and the African Christian Democratic Party spoke on the first day, the Pan Africanist Congress and the Democratic Alliance on the second, and the National Party (NP) and the ANC on days three and four respectively. The Inkatha Freedom Party appeared only later, on 6 September, and made it clear that it would not respond to further questions, nor return to any second hearing.

There was great interest in the presentations of the NP and the ANC in particular. Former President F.W. de Klerk ranged over the history of the changing policies of his party, emphasising the moves away from 'separate development' to the dismantling of apartheid and the establishment of the new South Africa. He argued that the NP government had tried to 'ascertain the truth and to secure the arrest of all perpetrators of serious violations of human rights, including members of the security forces'. He pointed to the establishment of commissions of inquiry aimed at exposing such violations, and to his government's change of direction in lifting the state of emergency in 1990 and entering into negotiations with the ANC.

Deputy President Thabo Mbeki presented the ANC submission, stressing the distinction between 'the forces of white minority domination on the one hand and the forces of national liberation and democracy on the other', making the point that the ANC's armed struggle had been based on a 'just cause'. Nevertheless, he argued, the party's insistence had always been that this struggle was only one of the four pillars of its strategy, and it had at the same time opposed terrorism and attacks on white civilians. The party would provide the TRC with information regarding any matter which could fall within the ambit of its mandate, and also with the proceedings of the Motsuenyane and Skweyiya commissions, which the ANC had itself set up to inquire into allegations of abuse and torture which had arisen in its camps in exile.

These hearings were met with general criticism in the media, which blamed the TRC for allowing the presentations to go largely unquestioned, instead of probing more deeply. The parties had not tabled their extensive submissions in advance of the hearing, so it had been impossible to study them and prepare questions. It was clear that the hearings had merely scratched the surface and these matters would have to be taken further. A second round of hearings was held in May 1997, during which the questioning was more intense, and the ANC representatives provided considerably more information. It was at this time that the heated exchanges took place between F.W. de Klerk and the chair and deputy chair of the TRC.

The security forces

A hearing into the role of the armed forces was held in Cape Town from 7 to 9 October 1997 in Cape Town. This shed light on actions of the armed wings of the ANC (MK, or Umkhonto we Sizwe) and the PAC (APLA, or the Azanian People's Liberation Army), as well as the South African Defence Force (SADF). The TRC Report provides extensive coverage of such actions, combining information from research as well as testimony at the hearing.[22]

Describing the effect on society of the wide reach of the SADF, Craig Williamson, the notorious security police spy, made the point that various civil institutions in the country had assisted the security forces: 'Our weapons, ammunition, uniforms, vehicles, radio and other equipment were all developed and provided by industry.' The banks provided credit, the chaplains prayed, and the media conveyed the propaganda.

The State Security Council, which under President P.W. Botha had been strengthened from 1979 onwards to formulate and execute national security policy, was the subject of a hearing in Johannesburg from 13 to 15 October 1997. The information that was made available demonstrated the extent to which the military forces were utilised for internal operations in support of the police, as well as the responsibility of the state for unlawful actions taken against people regarded as revolutionaries. Former National Party members of cabinet testified about the extent of their knowledge of the actions of the security forces during the apartheid era. Pik Botha, Adriaan Vlok, Leon Wessels and Roelf Meyer acknowledged that at the very least they had failed to question closely the actions of the security forces and the intelligence services, and they accepted political responsibility for this.

Institutional hearings

The commission was able to arrange for six institutional

or sectoral hearings, and received written submissions from hundreds of individuals and organisations. These submissions, like all the others received, form part of the material lodged in the TRC's Records Management Department, which were eventually transferred to the state archives[23] as part of all the commission's documentation.

Business and labour

As the TRC concludes in its Report, 'At the heart of the business and labour hearings lay the complex power relations of apartheid, the legacy of which continues to afflict the post-apartheid society. These include the consequences of job reservation, influx control, wages, unequal access to resources, migrant labour and the hostel system. Adjacent to these historic developments were industrial unrest, strikes and the struggle for the right to organise trade unions.'[24]

From 11 to 13 November 1997, some 30 verbal representations were made by employer bodies, trade unions, academic centres, and chambers of commerce and industry. Widely divergent perspectives emerged over the extent to which business as a whole had benefited from apartheid policies, or whether it had in fact been undermined by the high costs and lack of skilled labour prevalent under apartheid. Submissions from representatives of the business sector pointed to their efforts to influence the state to end migrant labour and to reform housing, land-ownership and skills training policies. Submissions from trade unions and academics stressed issues of extremely low wages, poor working conditions (especially in the mining and agricultural sector) and racial discrimination, and the fact that the business community had been involved in supporting the government's security and defence structures.

Individual contributors to the hearing, such as Bob Tucker, executive director of the Banking Council, supported the idea that the business sector should contribute towards 'reconstruction and development'. Professor Sampie Terreblanche proposed a wealth tax, which would contribute to reconciliation, social stability and economic growth. This would also provide a basis for restitution for those who had been impoverished through apartheid. At the conclusion of the hearing, the commission found that 'business was central to the economy that sustained the South African state during the apartheid years ... most [businesses] benefited from operating in a racially structured context.'[25] Furthermore, it identified the denial of trade union rights to black workers as a gross violation of human rights, and criticised the policies of specific sectors such as mining and agriculture.[26]

Prisons
The hearing into the prisons was held on 21 and 22 July 1997 in the Johannesburg Fort, an 'appropriate symbol

of political resistance' whose inmates had included Mahatma Gandhi and Nelson Mandela, as well as many apartheid detainees and prisoners, male and female. Joyce Seroke, a TRC committee member, had also been held there. Hugh Lewin and Tom Manthata were the committee members who spearheaded the arrangements: both of them had served prison sentences, Hugh in Pretoria Central and Tom on Robben Island.

'As an institution of the state, prisons – together with the police, the judiciary and the security apparatus – were an integral part of the chain of oppression of those who resisted apartheid.'[27] Statements submitted provided extensive evidence of gross violations of human rights suffered by prisoners, either in detention or while serving sentences.

The committee took the difficult decision to exclude three specific categories from this hearing:

(a) pass law offenders had formed a large proportion of the prison population during the 1960s and 1970s, being sentenced for offences that would not have been regarded as criminal almost anywhere else in the world. The pass laws had a devastating effect on the lives of thousands of South Africans, but they did not fall directly within the mandate of the TRC.

(b) farm prisons had provided cheap labour for farmers when African people arrested in terms of the pass laws were offered the option of 'volunteering' as farm workers instead of facing charges. In 1959 the government had amended the Prisons Act in order to provide for farms in this scheme to be considered as prisons, and made it an offence to publish anything about their conditions.

(c) detention without trial was estimated to have impacted on some 80,000 people between 1960 and 1990, up to 80 per cent of whom were eventually released without charge. The prisons had been a prime site for their detention, and frequently for their torture. Altogether 73 people had been recorded as having died while held under security legislation.[28] (Detentions without trial, and the deaths of those who had died while in detention, were matters covered in the general Human Rights Violations hearings.)

Themes highlighted for the hearing on prisons were the main political prisons (Robben Island (for blacks), Pretoria (for whites) and Barberton (for women)); the treatment of women prisoners; capital punishment; conditions in homeland prisons; health in prison; and conditions in the ANC 'camps' outside the country.

Some 25 witnesses appeared at the hearings, with the addition of several specialists: Paula McBride on capital punishment and conditions on death row, Judith van Heerden on health conditions in prisons, Benjamin Pogrund on restrictions on media coverage of prison conditions, and Golden Miles Bhudu of the South African Prisoners' Organisation for Human Rights (SAPOHR). The new Department of Correctional

Services, which had replaced the apartheid Department of Prisons, despite participating in several preliminary discussions, declined to be represented. The committee noted that this was a cause for regret, partly because it meant there was no official response to the testimonies presented and no perspective put forward about changes in prisons policy since 1994.

The testimonies offered at the hearing were harrowing, and they make difficult reading even today. They provided one account after another of appalling conditions, of solitary confinement for such long periods that those who suffered it never fully recovered, of torture and abuse and deaths, and of clear evidence that the Department of Prisons in the period under review was responsible for the use of cruel, degrading and inhuman forms of punishment.

Black prisoners suffered inferior quality of food, clothing, living conditions and medical care. Women prisoners endured particular cruelty in the form of threats against their families and of sexual harassment and brutality. White political prisoners were not protected from severe ill-treatment either. The hearings also gave attention to two testimonies concerning conditions in the ANC's detention camps in exile, including one by Joe Seremane, whose younger brother was executed in the ANC's Quatro camp in Angola.

The hearing on the health sector was held on 18 and 19 June 1977 in Cape Town. Wendy Orr and Fazel Randera (both medical doctors), Glenda Wildschut (a psychiatric nurse), and Hlengiwe Mkhize and Mapule Ramashala (specialists in mental health), all worked to make the hearing come about. Numerous submissions were received, of which the most bulky was that of the Health and Human Rights Project (HHRP), containing details about many misdemeanours, or failures to act appropriately, in various sectors, such as in the Defence Force or other state institutions.

The TRC Report on the hearing begins with an overview of the various ethical codes which have governed the medical profession 'from ancient times up until the present day'.[29] The commission noted that the 'greatest drawback of these codes and oaths is the difficulty of monitoring and enforcing compliance with them'. It commented on the situation of health professionals who were employed to provide medical care in prisons, but who found themselves under pressure to support the police and the prison authorities, resulting in negligence and a failure to follow internationally accepted guidelines of medical ethics and human rights. It highlighted the case of the district surgeons responsible for the care of Steve Biko when he was in detention in the Walmer police cells in Port Elizabeth. Biko's horrific death in 1977 was evidence of the callous negligence and 'improper conduct' on the part of state doctors, who failed to protect him from torture and inhumane conditions of detention.

The Report also listed numerous accounts of district surgeons who had failed to fulfil their moral duty as doctors: their failure to refer injured detainees to hospital, failure to enquire from detainees how they had incurred their injuries, asking the security police questions about such injuries instead; there was even an allegation that a district surgeon had been asked by the security police whether a detainee was fit to undergo further electric shock torture. It also referred to cases where doctors had reported false causes of death.

The death of Ashley Kriel in 1987 raised questions about how forensic information could be misused. The outcome of the inquest held at the time was that 'no blame' could be attached to the police involved in his shooting; it accepted the account of Jeffrey Benzien, the senior police officer involved. The explanation given had been that Benzien had tried to take a pistol away from Kriel and that in the ensuing scuffle Kriel had been fatally shot in the back. Several inconsistencies in the inquest finding account were pointed out. The case is once more under consideration (as at March 2016).

The Report also gave a comprehensive overview of state health organisations, including the medical service in the SADF, and the testimonies of doctors who had served in it. It pointed to the use of medical expertise in devising methods of interrogation and also to advising the security forces on the use of poisonous chemicals, methods of administering electric shock, and the development of weapons such as letter bombs.

The role of university medical schools and the systematic exclusion of black people from training opportunities in the profession were also examined, although it was recognised that in the later years of the period reviewed by the TRC there were some universities that spoke out against the inequities of apartheid medicine.

The Report covered the role of mental health professionals and of nurses, and other allied sectors such as physiotherapists, pharmacists, dentists and complementary practitioners. It pointed out the weaknesses of the professional organisations, such as the South African Medical and Dental Council, the Medical Association of South Africa, and the South African Nursing Council.[30] That this hearing was organised by members of the commission who themselves had specialised medical skills accounts for the considerable detail in the Report, and testifies to their passionate wish to see improved conditions in the future.

The media

The hearing on the media was held from 15 to 17 September 1997 at a large studio in the Johannesburg office of the SABC, which was made available free of charge. (The SABC had been under state control during apartheid.)[31] Topics covered included the racism experienced by black journalists as well as the racism within the structures of the media themselves; the role of spies in newsrooms and in senior positions; gender discrimination in employment opportunities; and state control over the media. Between 1950 and 1990 more than a hundred laws were introduced which affected the media, including the censoring and banning of publications and the threat of prosecution for disseminating subversive statements.

The TRC had two particular questions. Could the media under apartheid be held responsible for the perpetration of gross human rights violations? Moreover, to what extent could they be held responsible for creating a climate in which violations occurred unhindered? At the end of the hearing, the TRC found that 'With the notable exception of certain individuals, the mainstream newspapers and the SABC failed to report adequately on gross human rights violations. In so doing, they helped sustain and prolong the existence of apartheid'.[32] Max du Preez, former editor of *Vrye Weekblad*, told the hearing: 'If the mainstream newspapers and the SABC had reflected and followed up on all these confessions and revelations, every single one subsequently proved to have been true, the government would have been forced then to stop, to put a stop to the torture, the assassinations and the dirty tricks. It would have saved many, many lives.'[33]

Critics of the TRC have argued that although the commission 'set itself the task of finding a way to ensure that in the future ... a public broadcaster, unlike a state propaganda broadcaster, must be prepared to expose official malfeasance ... it did not keep its promise to recommend ways to avoid a repetition of these mistakes. Haste, confusion and a shortage of resources led to a hurried TRC report that did not address this.'[34] In fact, Volume 5 of the TRC's Report does include recommendations for amendments to legislation concerning revelation of sources and absence of interference from government, independence of the public broadcaster, support for a variety of media voices, self-regulation to deal with contacts between journalists and operatives of state intelligence or security agencies, and codes of conduct to prevent media workers from taking payment in exchange for information. It also recommended affirmative action policies to ensure a better balance among employees. It advocated that the media unions should strive for a unified strategy towards the industry.[35]

The legal community

This hearing, held from 27 to 29 October 1997 in Johannesburg, provided for members of the legal profession to testify about the way in which South African law had been administered, but it had to do so without the presence of the judges of the country. Five senior judges had indicated that they would make a statement but would not attend the hearings – former Chief Justice Michael Corbett; his successor, Judge Ismail Mahomed; Judge Arthur Chaskalson, president of the Constitutional Court; Judge Hennie van Heerden; and Judge Pius Langa. Written submissions were received from more than twenty judges, but none came to the hearing, despite the profound and publicly expressed disappointment of the TRC and Archbishop Tutu himself. The Commission's findings criticised the judiciary and the magistracy, although it recorded its view that there had been a minority of judges, lawyers, legal academics and students who had had the courage to oppose unjust laws.

The faith community

In his book *Chronicle of the Truth Commission,* Piet Meiring, the Johannesburg-based member of the Reparations and Rehabilitation Committee, recounts the meeting he had with the South African Council of Churches on 11 March 1997, when he suggested the concept of a public gathering where all the faith communities would testify. There was overwhelming support, and Bishop Dwane, president of the SACC, responded, 'If the churches do not lead the country in this, who will?'

The hearing took place in East London, from 17 to 19 November 1997, the last of the institutional hearings, and was preceded by a devotional service on Sunday, 16

November. Letters of invitation had been sent to over a hundred denominations and ecumenical organisations, including Muslim, Jewish, Hindu, Buddhist, Baha'i, Christian and African Independent churches. Meiring speaks of his relief and satisfaction when the Dutch Reformed Church agreed, and when almost at the last moment a delegation from the Zion Christian Church, the largest of the independent African churches, arrived. Leaders of all the major denominations testified, including bishops and theologians, the Chief Rabbi Cyril Harris, and leading members of Islam like Dr Farid Esack and Imam Rashied Omar. The hearing began and ended with contributions from women: Brigalia Bam of the South African Council of Churches, and Cathy Makhene, who spoke on behalf 'of all the women belonging to the various religions' and pointed out that 'all religions are heavily patriarchal. The fathers rule, while the mothers and daughters do all the work!'

The majority of the testimonies recognised that their communities had not done enough to counter the injustices of the past, had turned their backs on many opponents of apartheid, and had even sought to justify policies that were unjust. Many tendered apologies, and there was a strong thread of awareness that much work needed to be done to make amends. As Meiring concludes, 'in every submission the representatives of the various groups emphasized their resolution to walk the road of reconciliation.'[36]

Compulsory military service

The statements that poured into the TRC offices included those of individuals and families who had been part of the formal or semi-formal military conflict, around the borders of South Africa and within it. Great numbers of young men and women had been through military training, either by voluntarily going into exile in order to join the armed struggle of the liberation movements, or by being conscripted into the SADF. Many had been injured or killed in formal or informal battles. All had been engaged in an undeclared war between citizens of the same country.

The commission grappled with the question of where they fitted into the definitions of its mandate. Were they 'victims' or 'perpetrators', or neither? The discussions led into consideration of just war theories, international codes of conduct in military situations, and the vastly different ways in which the conflict had been seen by supporters and opponents of the government.

Eventually it was decided that a military combatant, trained, armed and equipped by a military structure (formal or informal), and acting under orders, could not be defined as a victim if he or she was killed or injured in a combat situation. Yet it seemed important to look more deeply into this aspect of the years of conflict, and a special hearing on conscription was convened.

It was held in Cape Town, on 21 and 22 July 1997. Archbishop Tutu said, 'We know that there have been different points of view about the sensitive issue of conscription and strong views expressed for and against the old SADF. Some hold very firmly to the view that South Africa was facing a total onslaught from the communist empire and its surrogates, and believed that they were constrained to defend South Africa against what they perceived as an atheistic, unchristian foe. Others believed, equally vehemently, that the enemy was not out there; that the border was here in our midst.'[37]

The hearing drew on a range of documents covering the militarisation of the whole society, the ways in which young white men were prepared from the age of 16 for their 'call-up' into the defence force, and the impact which the experience had on them. Submissions from political scientists, psychologists, army chaplains and former members of the SADF described the pressures on conscripts, and individual testimonies reflected on their own experiences. Some continued to defend the role of national service: 'We played a role in the struggle against communism ... against anarchy ... We are proud of our cultural heritage ... and we believe that our struggle was embedded in core values that we learnt in our families.' Schools and parents played a role in shaping these views, and women in particular became active in raising funds and providing moral and practical support for the SADF and its conscripted army.

On the other hand, submissions were made by representatives of the Committee on South African

War Resistance (COSAWR) and the End Conscription Campaign (ECC), covering the growth of resistance to military service. The individual experiences described 'two waves' of conscientious objectors – the first one in the 1970s, when objections were based primarily on religious grounds, and the second in the 1980s, when objections were more explicitly political.

A number of individuals spoke with courage about their own time in the SADF, the impact on them of waging war on the borders and of the actions of the troops in the townships within the country in the 1980s. Others had left the country to avoid conscription. Many continued to suffer from post-traumatic stress. One woman wrote to the commission about the death of her son and her struggle to come to terms with this loss. A footnote to this account is that after the hearing, the possibility arose of arranging a meeting between her and a young man who had been with her son when he died. Despite her grief, she obtained some comfort from learning at last what had happened.

Although no submissions were heard from the previous SADF, the role of the state was illustrated by Lieutenant Colonel Botha's account of a defence force project, Curamus Care for the Disabled. This includes treatment and aftercare for those with physical and psychological disabilities, and assistance with procedures such as applying for military pensions or for employment opportunities.

The hearing was a significant contribution to understanding some of the many issues faced by young white South Africans as they were forced to come to terms with the reality of the war being waged against compatriots. It portrayed the burden many of them carried during and after that time. It also demonstrated the enormous gulf between their experiences, and the support systems available to them in whatever choices they made, and the experiences of those who fought on the other side of the conflict.

These special hearings, together with accounts of special investigations undertaken by the commission into events – such as the death of Mozambican President Samora Machel, the *Helderberg* aeroplane crash, chemical and biological warfare, secret state funding for 'front' organisations, and political violence during the period of negotiations and transition (1990–4) – are extensively covered in the TRC Report. They provide insights into the conflicts that affected the lives of the individuals who contributed to the commission through their statements and amnesty applications. Without this understanding, reconciliation between former adversaries would be hard to achieve.

7

Challenges to be overcome

One of the greatest difficulties facing the commission was the sheer volume of work and the limited time in which to complete it. The task, which had been expected to take a year, with a possible extension to 18 months, had grown so great that repeated further extensions were required. By the end of 1997 there was still no end in sight: the Human Rights Violations and the Reparations and Rehabilitation committees were working at full tilt to complete findings and enable the process of notifying the victims of the outcome, so that the next step of applying for reparations could begin. The Amnesty Committee would clearly not complete its work on time: the appointment of additional committee members, made possible by yet another amendment to the legislation, was a help, but at times six panels were holding hearings at once, imposing an impossible burden on the staff. Additional logistical staff members were urgently needed. The investigators were still working on corroboration for both the Amnesty Committee and the Human Rights Violations Committee. Additional corroborators had to be brought in to strengthen this work. Everybody was working at full capacity.

At the same time, a number of people were leaving the commission to take up new or existing commitments, having anticipated that the TRC would be over by then. Shifting members from one committee to another helped to fill some gaps and to streamline the work. Plans were being made to close the regional offices by 31 March 1998, but the load in the Durban office was so great that it would have to stay open longer.

Criticism of the TRC mounted when the public hearings of the human rights violations ended while the amnesty hearings continued. Perpetrators were receiving amnesty, while the victims felt they had been left stranded without any responses and with no clarity about reparations.

Within the commission itself, these stresses had an impact on everyone involved. Over the months of working together, many strong bonds of friendship had been forged. Yet there were also unresolved tensions that came to the surface from time to time, or storms that came from outside to bedevil relationships. One of these arose from accusations against Dumisa Ntsebeza, a commissioner and head of the Investigation Unit, alleging that he had been implicated in the attack on the Heidelberg Tavern in Cape Town in 1993. This came to a dramatic head during the amnesty hearing in October 1997 for three APLA soldiers involved in the attack when he was pointed out by a witness as having been the owner and driver of a car involved. This was an extraordinary development. The witness had earlier made a statement to the effect that weapons had been placed in the same car on the night of the attack. Since Ntsebeza had been thus implicated, the Amnesty Committee was obliged to serve him with a formal notice informing him that he had the right to be present at the hearing and to be represented.

At the time, media attention was at its height and reports pointed to divisions and conflict within the Investigation Unit and the commission itself. There were suggestions that Ntsebeza should step aside from the TRC until the matter was resolved. An emergency meeting of the commission was convened, at which the commissioners decided to support Ntsebeza and not ask him to step aside. Within minutes, further drama erupted. The witness who had made the initial allegations had come to the TRC offices to apologise and to confess that his accusations were false and had been made under pressure. The entire affair, which was later investigated by Judge Richard Goldstone (who completely exonerated Ntsebeza), lent weight to the accumulating evidence of the arrogant use of lies, intimidation and other 'dirty tricks' employed by the security police.

Other difficult issues created differences of opinion among commissioners as the findings procedures moved on. One of them was how to handle the situation of active combatants in the struggle years – could they be defined as victims if they were killed or injured? This gave rise to discussion about whether those who had defended the apartheid government and those who had opposed it by military means could be regarded in the same way. Many MK guerrilla soldiers, such as Basil February and others involved in combat situations, were regarded as heroes by supporters of the liberation movements. Eventually it was agreed that active combatants, whether fighting to oppose or defend apartheid, if acting under orders of an established authority and engaged in combat, could not be found to be victims of gross human rights violations if they were injured or killed in such battle. This was by no means unanimous, and the final decision required negotiation and detailed explanation in the Final Report.

Another area of potential tension was the relations between the commissioners themselves and the entire staff, which needed to be sensitively managed. The commissioners worked hard, and carried responsibility, but they also received national and international recognition as well as generous remuneration. This came to a head at one point when an invitation was received from the Norwegian churches for commissioners to attend a period of retreat in Norway. A memorandum from staff conveyed their strong opposition to this special benefit being accepted, and it was recognised that it would have been insensitive for commissioners to take up this opportunity when it was not available to others.

By April 1998 most of the difficult decisions within the commission had been resolved. The ongoing anxiety about the unwillingness of the Inkatha Freedom Party to encourage its supporters to participate in the TRC processes had been overcome. The IFP had recognised that it would be to the detriment of possible victims of human rights violations if they did not make statements, for they would thus be excluded from the possibility of reparations. After this breakthrough, a large number of additional statement takers were appointed, drawn from a variety of organisations, and they contributed to a much fuller picture of events in the province of KZN. As a result the Durban office was still faced with 4,000 human rights violations findings to be made, and required additional resources and time.

Yet there were still three important matters which must be dealt with: the investigations into the parts played by former President P.W. Botha, Mrs Winnie Madikizela-Mandela and Dr Wouter Basson.

P.W. Botha

It was inconceivable that the TRC should ignore the role of P.W. Botha, Prime Minister since September 1978 and State President since 1984, who had been reluctantly forced to resign in August 1989. As head of state during the turbulent 1980s, he surely bore the overall responsibility for the gross violations of human rights which his government had sanctioned during those years.

In his retirement he was angrily opposed to the TRC, but Archbishop Tutu went to see him in George in October 1996 and they had a relatively cordial conversation, although he remained obdurately opposed to appearing before the commission. Various efforts were made to draw him in, including a set of questions sent to him in February 1997, which he had indicated he would consider, but no answers were received. Eventually, with time running out, the TRC issued a subpoena for him to appear at the hearing on the State Security Council. This was withdrawn on the grounds of his ill-health, but a second subpoena was issued. When he refused to appear, he was charged with contempt and appeared in the George magistrate's court on 23 February 1998. The matter was adjourned until April and then to June. In August he was found guilty of contravening sections of the Promotion of National Unity and Reconciliation Act, and sentenced to a fine or 12 months' imprisonment. This was set aside when an appeal was made on technical grounds, based on the date on which the notice had been served on him. The TRC decided not to appeal further. It had succeeded in raising the questions to be placed before him, and ensuring that he faced them in court, and it was able to make extensive findings, concluding in the Final Report that he had 'contributed to and facilitated a climate in which gross violations of human rights could and did occur, and as such is accountable for such violations'.[38]

Winnie Madikizela-Mandela

Nomzamo Winnie Madikizela-Mandela has been a prominent figure for decades in South Africa, a social worker and political activist, and leader in the ANC. She married Nelson Mandela in 1958, and for most of the next thirty years was the target of actions against her by the security arms of the state. She was banned, restricted, exiled to Brandfort, held in detention in solitary confinement for many months, charged with a variety of contraventions, and constantly harassed. The full story of her life and of the impact that these experiences had on her has yet to be told.

By June 1988 she was once again living in Soweto, in a time of great conflict and violence. She gathered around herself a group of young men who came to be known as the Mandela United Football Club and who acted as protectors for her. They became increasingly feared for their suspected acts of assault and other abuses. In 1989 it emerged that they had been responsible for the abduction of four youths, one of whom was found killed. Jerry Richardson, the 'coach' of the football club, was charged with and convicted of the murder of Stompie

Seipei, and Madikizela-Mandela was implicated in the abduction and assault of the four. On appeal she was found guilty of the kidnapping, though not the assault.

The TRC held a hearing into the role of the Mandela United Football Club, which took place in Johannesburg over nine days, opening on 24 November 1997. Among those who testified were several parents who were desperate to know what had happened to their children, people who spoke about having themselves been assaulted by Madikizela-Mandela or in her presence, and the two people who had been jailed for such offences and had provided an alibi for her, who now said they had lied to protect her. Allegations were made that she had ordered the deaths of a number of people, including the prominent doctor Abu-Baker Asvat, who had been called by Madikizela-Mandela to treat the youths assaulted by her thugs. Others who spoke were Bishop Peter Storey and the Reverend Paul Verryn (now Bishop Verryn, from whose house in Soweto the youths had been abducted), and several members of the Mandela Crisis Committee, which had been set up by the ANC to try to deal with the problem at the time.

Archbishop Tutu presided over the hearing. When Madikizela-Mandela came to testify, she was led through hours of questioning, during which she evaded all responsibility and said the accusations were all mere fabrications. In a dramatic end to the proceedings, an emotional Archbishop Tutu spoke of the close relationship between his family and the Mandela family, and their long history in the struggle. He acknowledged her role in history, and yet begged her to admit in public that 'something went horribly wrong', and to say sorry. In the hush that followed, she said to the family of Dr Asvat and to Stompie's mother 'how deeply sorry I am' for 'those painful years when things went horribly wrong'.[39]

The long hearing had exposed a great deal, but there were no satisfactory answers to the questions that had been raised. The apology without the full truth was not enough, and further investigations should be pursued.

Dr Wouter Basson

Dr Wouter Basson was the head of Project Coast, South Africa's secret chemical and biological warfare (CBW) project. This was a research programme established formally in 1983 to lead the search for CBW-related poisons, ostensibly for defensive purposes, but later for offensive capability. They included compounds that could be used in riot control as well as drugs and poisons for purposes of assassinations. One who was almost killed by poisons placed on his clothing in 1989 was the Reverend Frank Chikane, general secretary of the South African Council of Churches and later director-general in the Office of the President. In 1991 President F.W. de Klerk ordered the end of the production of lethal chemical agents, and the next year Project Coast was officially closed. Dr Basson was arrested in 1997 on charges of possession and attempted sale of 1,000 Ecstasy tablets. Two related amnesty applications opened the door for investigations, and hearings were held in June and July 1998. Basson himself refused to apply for amnesty.

The National Intelligence Agency, the Office for Serious Economic Offences, and the office of the Attorney-General were also interested in pursuing the matter, and when the TRC first decided to issue a subpoena to Basson, they intervened. In the meantime, the commission proceeded with its investigations and found it had opened a can of worms. The project, it seemed, had involved huge expenses, not least from international travel and exposure to CBW facilities in other countries, and there was evidence of fraud and self-enrichment of individuals.

The TRC did not have the capacity to do more than uncover some of these aspects. It found among other things that the programme was 'in the hands of one person, Dr Basson' and that his superiors were 'grossly negligent in approving programmes and allocating large sums of money' for its activities. It referred to the front companies that had been established, and it found that the programme would not have been possible without some level of international cooperation and support.[40]

After the work of the TRC, the state continued to investigate, and in October 1999 Basson went on trial for 67 charges, including drug possession, fraud, conspiracy to murder, and murder. The judge in the case reduced the number to 46, and after many witnesses gave evidence, Basson himself responded in July 2001. In April 2002 he was acquitted of all the charges, and a chorus of criticism ensued. The state appealed to the Supreme Court of Appeal (SCA) against the judgment, and when this was rejected, it turned to the Constitutional Court. The Concourt ruled against some of the aspects of the SCA judgment, thereby allowing the prosecuting authorities to open new proceedings against Basson, but this has not yet happened. Basson has been free to pursue his medical profession since that time, except for the fact that he was found guilty in December 2013 by the Health Professions Council of South Africa of unethical conduct for his role in the CBW project.

The final hurdles

There were two final legal obstacles to overcome before the TRC Report could be presented to President Mandela.

The Report had been in piece-by-piece preparation from late 1997, and from January 1998 every meeting of the TRC dealt with draft chapters as they were produced. These had usually been prepared by the Research Department with contributions from the different sectors of the TRC. Chapters were distributed in advance, comments received, and finally confirmed and adopted. In July and August numerous meetings were convened only a few days apart in order to complete this process.

Usually there was little dispute, but the commissioner Wynand Malan voiced his concern that there was insufficient contribution overall to national unity and reconciliation, and too much focus on apartheid itself. Eventually, Malan wrote a minority report, to the great disappointment of the commission as a whole.

The Report was ready for publication in mid-October, with the printers standing by to produce the hundreds of copies required. The morning of 29 October 1998 saw the commissioners and many other members of the TRC, as well as a large contingent of national and international journalists, gathered in Pretoria, anxiously awaiting the time of the presentation of the Final Report to President Mandela.

However, two late legal challenges to TRC findings could have prevented the publication of the Report in time. One of them had been settled by agreement, and the verdict of the Cape High Court would that very morning decide the outcome of the other. Cellular telephones were much in evidence as the hours passed.

In Cape Town, Judge John Hlophe was considering an application of the ANC which had arisen from the notification sent to it by the TRC on 24 August 1998, setting out as required the intention to make certain findings against it, and inviting the ANC to respond – either at a hearing or by making written submissions within 15 days (i.e. by 8 September). No response had been received to the notice, although there was correspondence seeking an extension to the deadline and requesting an audience with the commission.

This had led to several discussions within the commission (now led by acting chairperson Dumisa Ntsebeza), with a small number of commissioners present in Cape Town. It would be extremely difficult to grant an extension of the deadline in view of the desperate race to have the Report published on time, but in fact an absolutely final date was offered of 5 October. At the same time the commission agreed that it would be improper to agree to an audience with the ANC to discuss the proposed findings. No other party or individual had been granted such an opportunity, and the same practice must be followed for all. Commissioners who had not been present endorsed this view.

The 5 October deadline passed, and the Report was finalised, including the findings against the ANC. On 19 October the ANC finally made its submission, and commissioners met once again to decide how to proceed. On 26 October the general secretary of the ANC was informed that the submission had arrived too late to be considered. A number of commissioners had read the submission, and their view was that the arguments raised in it had in any event largely been addressed within the Report.

The ANC responded, indicating its dissatisfaction and demanding an assurance from all commissioners that they had properly considered its submission – to which the TRC replied reiterating its position. The ANC then brought an urgent application to the Cape High Court for an interdict restraining the commission from publishing any portion of its Report that implicated the ANC in gross violations of human rights before it had considered the ANC submission.

The court dismissed the application, finding that the commission had been entitled to establish the procedure for receiving submissions within a specified period, that the ANC had failed to meet the deadlines given, and that because its 19 October submission was extensive and contained serious allegations regarding the commission's competence, integrity and bona fides, it would have been unreasonable to expect it to discuss and deliberate on it in the short time available.

The court's decision was instantly reported to Pretoria, where the presentation of the report to President Mandela was able to proceed. His courtesy and that of Archbishop Tutu ensured the dignity of the occasion, but the atmosphere of celebration that could have prevailed had been dimmed.

The other application for an interdict was brought by former President F.W. de Klerk, who, on 1 September 1998, had been sent the requisite notification of findings contemplated against him. Objections were received from De Klerk, but the commission decided to confirm and publish the findings, so on 26 October De Klerk's lawyers filed an application with the Cape High Court for an order to interdict the TRC from making the intended findings; from including any of the intended findings in the Report to be submitted to President Mandela; and from submitting the Report should it contain any of the findings.

The TRC's own lawyers' advice was to avoid risking the interdict, and to enter into an agreement not to publish the findings in order not to delay the presentation of the Report. The findings had already been printed, but it was agreed that the page would be blacked out in every copy, and another way to deal with De Klerk's objections would be sought.

After the main body of the TRC had gone into suspension, it became the task of the Amnesty Committee to enter into discussions with De Klerk. An agreement was reached between the parties that the TRC would make a revised finding (which is published in full in Vol. 6 of the Report, one of the two volumes that make up the 'codicil' which was presented to President Thabo Mbeki on 21 March 2003). However, this finding was never made an order of court, as it was never put to the full commission (which had been in suspension since October 1998) and had therefore never been discussed, accepted or rejected.

With these two legal challenges behind it, the commission was able to present its Report. Only the Amnesty Committee was now left in existence, and it would still have to deal with further complaints and applications relating to the TRC's findings and procedures, in addition to challenges to its own amnesty-related decisions.

Both the Inkatha Freedom Party (IFP) and a group of former SADF generals made formal complaints to the Office of the Public Protector about what they claimed to be disparate treatment of themselves by the commission. The commission responded fully to the allegations and the Public Protector neither took nor recommended any action against the commission.

The IFP, together with its leader Chief Mangosuthu Buthelezi, also brought an application before the Cape High Court in December 1998. In response to the notification that the TRC contemplated making findings against them, they had on 24 August submitted a comprehensive submission. However, the TRC had proceeded to make the findings, which had been published in the Report. Now in their application, they declared that they regarded these findings as defamatory, unwarranted and unjustified. The order they sought was to compel the commission to provide all the information collected and received upon which it had made its findings.

On 15 December 1998 Judge Dennis Davis dismissed the application with costs, but the applicants sought and received leave to appeal to the Constitutional Court. The matter was set down for 9 November 2000, but before that date the parties agreed to settle. The commission agreed to provide access to the requested information by 1 March

2001, on condition that appropriate measures were taken to guard the confidentiality of statements which had been made to the commission. This decision was taken in the knowledge that the Promotion of Access to Information Act was due to be gazetted on 15 September 2000, and this legislation would have entitled the applicants to obtain the information they were seeking.

Even after all of this litigation, the IFP and Chief Buthelezi instituted review proceedings against the findings of the commission on 20 October 2000, and just before the final codicil was to be published they interdicted the publication on the grounds that the terms of the settlement had not been met. A settlement was finally reached at a hearing on 29 January 2003. In terms of the agreement, the TRC accepted the validity of some of the criticisms of the applicants and agreed to publish an appendix to the Report reflecting the views of the IFP and Minister Buthelezi.

All of these obstacles, legal and administrative, demonstrate how difficult it is for any transitional justice mechanism to arrive at conclusions that will stand up to careful scrutiny and also contribute to a greater recognition of the injustices and abuses of the past. The TRC's findings were criticised and challenged on all sides of the political spectrum. This placed it under pressure to respond, but it was also an indication that it had preserved its independence and had required accountability from all participants.

8

Truth, justice, reparations
Can they bring reconciliation?

Since 1983, some thirty truth commissions have been established around the world, and many countries are still trying to find ways to set up similar structures in fragile societies emerging from years of internal conflict.

In Argentina the National Commission on the Disappearance of Persons (CONADEP) was established in 1983 and delivered its report in 1984. Commissions were also set up in Chile (the National Commission on Truth and Reconciliation, which completed its work in 1991) and El Salvador (the Commission on the Truth, completed in 1993), and the term 'truth commissions' became part of the terminology of transitional justice. By the time South Africa came to set up its own, there were many lessons to be learned and South Africans made contacts with individuals who had been closely involved with these processes elsewhere.

The successful and mostly peaceful outcome of the

1994 elections, and the prior agreements reached during the CODESA negotiations, gave South Africa a stable platform on which to build its own transitional justice programme, without fear of a military or right-wing coup. When it came to establish the Truth and Reconciliation Commission, the government felt sufficiently secure to grant it much wider powers than those in other countries had enjoyed. The commissions in El Salvador, Chile and Argentina were given no powers of subpoena or search and seizure. There was no link in these countries to any amnesty arrangement, and so they could offer no incentive to obtain perpetrators' stories but had to rely on investigations and continuing pressure, as well as the voluntary cooperation of individuals invited to give testimony.

South Africa's commission had the benefit of the experience of these countries, as well as the support of the new government. It had the capacity to operate in the public eye through its open hearings and the support of the media. Another advantage was the offer of amnesty to draw in the testimonies of perpetrators, whose statements contributed to the uncovering of the truth. The individual applications for amnesty were subject to investigation and to various conditions. The provision for swift decision-making on the granting of amnesty, although it created problems for the commission, was a contrast to countries such as Chile, where a self-amnesty law had been passed by the military government before the democratic elections.

The process of establishing the South African TRC, with contributions from civil society, open debate in Parliament, and a transparent mechanism for the appointment of commissioners, also differed from that of many other commissions. Some of the latter were put in place by presidential decree without public debate, or by a negotiated peace accord. Some do not even refer to the aspect of reconciliation. In Argentina, for example, the well-known mothers and grandmothers who continue to demonstrate once a week outside the presidential palace, seeking information about their children, and demanding the prosecution of perpetrators, have no wish to talk about reconciliation. 'We do not want to forgive, we want justice.'

Transitional justice is never good enough – it is always a compromise born out of past conflict and injustice. It has to be measured against the alternative – ongoing destructive conflict, which has the possibility of destroying many of the opportunities for development that the majority of people need. It also has to be balanced with whatever measures are possible for restorative justice, in the knowledge that in many societies devastated by their previous experiences, there are not sufficient resources to offer individual reparations.

As Nomfundo Walaza, who was the director of the Trauma Centre for Survivors of Violence and Torture in Cape Town, has said, 'If we are to accept that at the core of the TRC's formation was a national gain (a political settlement and avoidance of bloodshed), then we have to face the unfortunate reality of a conflict between the interests of victims and survivors on the one hand and those of the nation as a whole on the other.'[41]

Transitional justice does imply the sacrifice of the rights of individuals for the benefit of the wider community, and it will only succeed if that benefit is indeed translated into reality for the majority of the population. How to measure that benefit is difficult as the years pass and a new generation looks back on the South African experience. If one considers the institutional and sectoral hearings of the TRC and the recommendations made there, for example, with regard to conditions in prisons or on the question of military conscription, it is possible to see how much progress has been achieved. Prisons are still dreadful places, hopelessly overcrowded and dangerously violent, but they are not places where secret torture can take place. Military conscription is a thing of the past. There have been some major improvements in the delivery of health services. Education, skills training and work opportunities still need urgent attention, as does the provision of adequate housing and access to land. While freedom of expression and the independence of the judiciary require constant vigilance, they now have the protection of the Constitution.

Every transitional justice arrangement is the outcome of a compromise and depends on the balance of power at the time and the particular circumstances of each case. By definition, it is a way of relinquishing some form of retributive justice in exchange for truth, and in the hope of peace and democracy. While some may regard it as a sham designed to take away the right to justice, others in countries ravaged by seemingly irreconcilable conflicts yearn for the day when they can embark on such a process. Burundi, for example, has long been considering a truth commission, and had reached the point of creating the structures and appointing the commissioners, but political disagreements have brought them to a halt. A study of 15 cases of mass political violence from around the world, including Zanzibar, Spain, the Ukraine and Algeria, records events where 'there were no trials, no truth commissions, no acknowledgement, no accountability'.[42]

A more sober assessment of the South African experience, as well as that of other countries, demonstrates that even if a good deal of truth is revealed and reparations are made, reconciliation cannot be achieved only by transitional structures, even if they help to lay a foundation of widely acknowledged truth. Reparations policies are important, and must be carefully planned and acknowledged by victims, and also by the wider society, as being just and able to be implemented rapidly. In societies where the economy is fragile or has been damaged by the years of warfare, the possibilities may be limited, but mechanisms to improve the quality of people's lives are still necessary.

The most successful way to compensate for the injustice of the past is to build stable, just democracies where the rights of all are equally respected and protected, where institutions and civil society have the means to ensure accountability from the state and its officials, and where attention is given to socio-economic justice and equity. One of the ways of achieving this is to keep holding government (and perpetrators) accountable, and to maintain a close watch on the way in which events are memorialised and represented. For this purpose, centres of memory, archives and state records should be available for historical research. Films, books, plays and poetry as well as other art forms can portray some of the events and lessons to be taken from these sources in a more accessible format.

The vision of the South African TRC, like that of other similar commissions before and after it, included the necessity to ensure that never again would the country be governed without the protection of the rule of law, the right of all persons equally to the safeguards of impartial courts, and to all the civil and human rights guaranteed by a constitution. One of the means to reach this goal is an understanding of history, and the protection of the records which ensure that history is told. The TRC was at times accused of not paying sufficient attention to history or of trying to rewrite history. Its own Report will be subject to the examination of historians, and provides one of the sources on which they will draw. Furthermore, the TRC's vast records of statements, investigations and discussions exist in a variety of forms – paper documentation, electronic recordings, public broadcasts – all forming part of a unique archive.

At the same time, the commission was acutely aware that under the previous government there had been a great deal of covert activity, that a culture of secrecy was a component of the security establishment, and that much history remained hidden. During its own investigations, it discovered that many important records had been destroyed, sometimes even as its inquiries were taking place. Part of its specific mandate had been 'to determine what articles have been destroyed by any person in order to conceal violations of human rights or acts associated with a political objective'. For this very reason, the TRC recommended that its complete archive be stored in the National Archives, and that resources should be made available for it to be processed in such a way as to make it available for future research.

The TRC also recommended specifically that the state should undertake a comprehensive analysis of apartheid-era security establishment records, and that these should be placed in the custody of the National Archives. There are many questions about whether any progress has been made in this regard. In 2001, for example, the South African History Archive revealed through court action that Military Intelligence had hidden from the TRC the vast majority of its surviving apartheid-era records. It should not be necessary for organisations or individuals to have to resort to the courts in order to make certain that such important historical records are not concealed.

Twenty years after the TRC, there is not enough public awareness of its work, its successes and failings. The full account of its proceedings should be made accessible, in a variety of ways: centres of memory where members of the public could have access to information; the collection of oral histories to supplement the accounts that were brought to the commission; and further research and analysis to ensure that what is taught in schools and tertiary institutions adds to the general understanding of the transitional process to which the TRC contributed.

The commission's Report includes a final seventh volume, which is a full list of the names of all the people found to have been victims of gross violations of human rights. This at least is a record in which the descendants or family of those persons can find some brief details of what happened to them. It is part of the task of acknowledgement of past sufferings. Very few truth commissions in the world have been able to publish the names of those found to be responsible for abuses; South Africa did publish many, but was prevented from naming others.

In the end, the real heroes of the TRC process are the victims, those who stepped forward to make the process of transitional justice work. If they had not come to testify, the South African TRC would have been a disastrous failure.

In Buenos Aires there is an organisation called Memoria Abierta (Open Memory), which keeps records of those who disappeared during the military dictatorship and continues to try to find evidence about them. In some ways it is like the Khulumani organisation in South Africa: both continue to hold their governments accountable for the unfinished work of the commissions they established. South Africa's Institute for Justice and Reconciliation, and other organisations which keep the historical archives alive, have taken up aspects of the work that still needs to be done. This includes bodies that have lobbied the government on behalf of victims: the Trauma Centre, the Centre for the Study of Violence and Reconciliation, ACCORD, the KZN Programme for the Survivors of Violence, Khulumani and others.

It is interesting to note that in Argentina, more than 30 years since the publication of the CONADEP report, new discoveries continue to be made, and some perpetrators have voluntarily confessed to the part they played in assassinations, or the disposal of bodies during the time of the 'dirty war'.

In South Africa, the National Prosecuting Authority houses the Missing Persons Task Team, which continues to look for and find places where bodies were illicitly buried, and to exhume them so that the remains can be returned to their families and buried with dignity.

It has recovered 102 bodies to date, of which 89 have been identified and returned to their families for burial. The remainder are awaiting DNA test results or other forensic examination results.[43]

Memorials have been created in many parts of the country, at particular sites of memory. There are lessons to be learned within the archive, for South Africa itself and for other countries engaged in similar transitions.

The TRC taught us that if reconciliation is to be achieved, there are several steps which must be taken: acknowledgement of harm done, apology and atonement.

Acknowledgement can take the form of an individual recognition of responsibility and a telling of the full truth, or it can come from a recognised authority such as the state. It can refer to acts committed or to involuntary benefits accrued from unjust situations.

Apology too can be made by one person for his or her acts, or by an organisation or association of persons. It can also refer to regret for injustices that were not committed by the person or group, but that resulted in their unfair advantage.

Atonement comprises the steps to be taken to offer redress: these can consist of improvement of socio-economic conditions, or of restoration of dignity, of contributing to the removal of barriers of class, race, ethnicity, gender and language. Individual pledges of restitution can open many possibilities of creating new relationships.[44] On a national basis, restitution requires a commitment from the state and the development of specific programmes, in consultation with those who suffered and continue to experience injustice, and with participation from those who derived advantage from it.

Atonement also consists of the delivery of justice. Whereas amnesty can be offered as part of a bridge to a new society, it cannot be allowed to offer impunity to those who do not fulfil its criteria. As demonstrated by the case of Nokuthula Simelane, there remains much work to be done.

'Why revisit old hurts?' I asked in the first chapter of this book. The answer is that unless they are attended to, they will not heal.

Notes

1 The legislation which established the TRC uses the word 'victim'
to define a person who has suffered a gross violation of her or
his rights. This is a contested term, with the word 'survivor'
being generally preferred. I have used the word 'victim' (without
quotation marks) throughout this book in order to conform to the
legal definition, but I acknowledge and support the right of those
who endured such abuse to be recognised as survivors.

2 TRC Report, vol. 1, p. 175.

3 The proceedings of the conferences were published in Alex
Boraine, Janet Levy and Ronel Scheffer (eds.), *Dealing with the
Past: Truth and Reconciliation in South Africa*, IDASA, 1994, and
Alex Boraine and Janet Levy (eds.), *The Healing of a Nation?*,
Justice in Transition, 1995.

4 Desmond Tutu, Alex Boraine, Mary Burton, Chris de Jager,
Bongani Finca, Sisi Khampepe, Richard Lyster, Wynand Malan,
Khoza Mgojo, Hlengiwe Mkhize, Dumisa Ntsebeza, Wendy Orr,
Denzil Potgieter, Mapule Ramashala, Fazel Randera, Yasmin
Sooka and Glenda Wildschut.

5 The committee members appointed to join the Human Rights
Violations Committee were Russell Ally, June Crichton, Mdu
Dlamini, Virginia Gcabashe, Pumla Gobodo-Madikizela, Ilan
Lax, Hugh Lewin, Judith 'Tiny' Maya, Motho Mosuhli, Ntsikelelo
Sandi and Joyce Seroke. Those who joined the Reparations and
Rehabilitation Committee were S'mangele Magwaza, Tom

Manthata, Piet Meiring, Mcebisi Xundu and Mandisa Olifant.

6 There are some discrepancies in the total numbers quoted in various publications, including Vol. 1 of the TRC Report, which at p. 269 gives the total as 7,127. However, it seems that the figure of 7,116 cited by Martin Coetzee, executive secretary to the committee, is the final tally.

7 TRC Report, Vol. 5, pp. 24–5 gives a full list of the 76 hearings.

8 TRC Report, Vol. 1, p. 421.

9 Karin Chubb and Lutz van Dijk, *Between Anger and Hope: South Africa's Youth and the Truth and Reconciliation Commission*, Witwatersrand University Press, 2001. See also the films *The Wynberg Seven*, by Siona O'Connell; *The Gugulethu Seven* by Lindy Wilson; and *Between Joyce and Remembrance* and *Black Christmas* by Mark Kaplan. Also music: *Rewind: A Cantata for Voice, Tape and Testimony*, composed by Philip Miller, 2007.

10 Max du Preez, *A Rumour of Spring*, Zebra Press, Cape Town, 2013, pp. 17–18.

11 J. Sarkin, *Carrots and Sticks: The TRC and the South African Amnesty Process*, Intersentia, Antwerp and Oxford, 2004, p. 154.

12 Dumisa Ntsebeza has argued that the TRC erred in accepting the suggestion from the military leadership that a 'nodal point' be established through which all military information would be channelled to the commission. This amounted to the establishment of a 'gatekeeper' for all information and documents released by the military. T. Bell and D. Ntsebeza, *Unfinished Business: South Africa, Apartheid and Truth*, Redworks, Cape Town, 2001, p. 262.

13 Sarkin, *Carrots and Sticks*, p. 264.

14 TRC Report, Vol. 6, p. 182.

15 The name of the court refers to the pre-1994 provincial arrangement, as the process of restructuring the court system in the new provinces was still under way.

16 Vusi Pikoli, previous Director of the NPA, tabled an affidavit to this effect. See the Media Release by the Simelane family and their legal advisers, 9 February 2016, supplied by Advocate Howard Varney.

17 I am indebted for much of this information about the amnesty decisions to Howard Varney, Hugo van der Merwe and Jeremy Sarkin.

18 These proposals were dealt with in considerable detail in the TRC's Final Report, in Vol. 5.

19 SACTJ comprises the Centre for the Study of Violence and Reconciliation, the Human Rights Media Centre, the Institute for Justice and Reconciliation, the International Center for Transitional Justice, the Khulumani Support Group, the Legal Resources Centre and the South African History Archives.

20 Pablo de Greiff, 'Reparations and Development', in A. Boraine and S. Valentine (eds.), *Transitional Justice and Human Security*, ICTJ, Cape Town, 2006.

21 TRC Report, Vol. 4, p. 1.

22 TRC Report, Vol. 2, pp. 325–99.

23 A list of these can be found in the TRC Report, vol. 4, pp. 5–17.

24 Vol. 4, p. 18.

25 Vol. 4, p. 56.

26 Vol. 4, p. 58.

27 Vol. 4, p. 199.

28 TRC Report, Vol. 4, pp. 201–2.

29 TRC Report, Vol. 4, pp. 158–9.

30 TRC Report, Vol. 4, p. 145.

31 TRC Report, Vol. 4, p. 168.

32 TRC Report, Vol. 4. p. 189.

33 TRC Report, Vol. 4, p. 188.

34 John Matisonn, *God, Spies and Lies*, Missing Ink, Cape Town, 2015, pp. 286 and 290.

35 TRC Report, Vol. 5, pp. 341–3.

36 Piet Meiring, *Chronicle of the Truth Commission*, Carpe Diem, Vanderbijlpark, 1999, p. 285.

37 TRC Report, Vol. 4, p. 220.

38 TRC Report, Vol. 5, p. 225.

39 A. Boraine, *A Country Unmasked*, OUP, Cape Town, 2000, p. 252.

40 TRC Report, Vol. 2, pp. 521–3.

41 N. Walaza, 'Insufficient Healing and Reparation', in C. Villa-Vicencio and W. Verwoerd (eds.), *Looking Back, Reaching Forward*, UCT Press, Cape Town, 2000.

42 H. Adam (ed.), *Hushed Voices: Unacknowledged Atrocities of the 20th Century*, Berkshire Academic Press, Luton, 2011, p. vii.

43 Personal communication from Madeleine Fullard, Director of the Missing Persons Task Team, 23 June 2016.

44 As, for example, the work undertaken in Worcester by the Restitution Foundation.

Select bibliography

There are hundreds of books, journal articles and academic theses about truth commissions and the South African TRC. I have learned a great deal from many of them, but have listed here only those which have accompanied me most closely in the preparation of this book.

Adam, Heribert, *Hushed Voices: Unacknowledged Atrocities of the 20th Century*, Luton, 2011

Boraine, Alex, *A Country Unmasked: Inside South Africa's Truth and Reconciliation Commission*, Cape Town, 2000

Boraine, Alex, *What's Gone Wrong? On the Brink of a Failed State*, Cape Town and Johannesburg, 2014

Boraine, Alex, Levy, Janet and Scheffer, Ronel, *Dealing with the Past: Truth and Reconciliation in South Africa*, Cape Town, 1994

Boraine, Alex and Levy, Janet (eds.), *The Healing of a Nation?*, Cape Town, 1995

Boraine, Alex and Valentine, Sue (eds.), *Transitional Justice and Human Security*, Cape Town, 2006

Chubb, Karin and Van Dijk, Lutz, *Between Anger and Hope: South Africa's Youth and the Truth and Reconciliation Commission*, Johannesburg, 2001

Cole, Catherine, *Performing South Africa's Truth Commission: Stages of Transition*, Bloomington, 2010

Doxtader, Eric (ed.), *Provoking Questions: An Assessment of the Truth and Reconciliation Commission's Recommendations and Their Implementation*, Cape Town, 2005

Du Preez, Max, *A Rumour of Spring: South Africa after 20 Years of Democracy*, Cape Town, 2013

Folb, Peter and Gould, Chandre, *Project Coast: Apartheid's Chemical and Biological Warfare Programme*, Cape Town and Geneva, 2002

James, Wilmot and Van de Vijver, Linda (eds.), *After the TRC: Reflections on Truth and Reconciliation in South Africa*, Cape Town, 2000

Klaas, Eric, *Guguletu Seven: The local version*, Cape Town, 2009

Matisonn, John, *God, Spies and Lies*, Cape Town, 2015

Meiring, Piet, *Chronicle of the Truth Commission*, Vanderbijlpark, 1999

Orr, Wendy, *From Biko to Basson*, Saxonwold, 2000

Sarkin, Jeremy, *Carrots and Sticks: The TRC and the*

South African Amnesty Process, London/Antwerp, 2004

Van der Merwe, Hugo, 'Prosecutions, pardons and amnesty: the trajectory of transitional accountability in South Africa', in *Critical Perspectives in Transitional Justice*, ed. by Nicola Palmer, Phil Clark and Danielle Granville, Cambridge/Antwerp/Portland, 2013

Villa-Vicencio, Charles, *Walk with Us and Listen: Political Reconciliation in Africa*, Cape Town, 2009

Villa-Vicencio, Charles and Verwoerd, Wilhelm (eds.), *Looking Back, Reaching Forward: Reflections on the Truth and Reconciliation Commission of South Africa*, Cape Town, 2000

Acknowledgements

Gathering the information for this book has increased my knowledge about the TRC, reminded me of the extraordinary experience of being part of it, and developed my understanding of how it fits into the worldwide quest for transitional justice.

I wish to acknowledge all those who have recorded and analysed the work that was done, as well as those who undertook the tasks and continue to carry forward the 'unfinished business'.

Most particularly, I should like to pay tribute to my colleagues on the TRC, including every member of the staff in all the regions, and those who stepped forward to assist in any way. The TRC Report made an attempt to list all the staff (Vol. 1, pp. 262–6), but there will have been others who joined at different stages. Every aspect of the work was made possible by their dedication, and they can never be sufficiently rewarded. Thanks to the efforts of the CEO, Biki Minyuku, they did at least receive their own specially produced (and beautifully illustrated) commemorative book, sponsored by USAID, which also contains a list of staff members (*Moments of Truth: The Truth and Reconciliation Commission at Work*, Cape Town, 1998).

The organisations and individuals who remain dedicated to the pursuit of justice and the quest for further knowledge, who have kept working and thinking and writing for the past two decades, bring a measure of relief for those who still seek answers. They sustain pressure on the authorities, they contribute to the world's awareness of what transitional justice means. They include the Centre for the Study of Violence and Reconciliation, the Institute for Justice and Reconciliation, the International Center for Transitional Justice, the Khulumani Support Group, the South African History Archives, the Human Rights Media Centre, the Healing of Memories Institute, the Trauma Centre for Survivors of Violence and Torture, as well as others internationally and nationally who provide support to victims of abuse.

I am very grateful to all those who have helped me with information, with greater clarity of understanding, with last-minute answers to questions, and with comments on earlier versions of the book. They are Charles Villa-Vicencio, Howard Varney, Jeremy Sarkin, Madeleine Fullard, Hugo van der Merwe, Marjorie Jobson and

Annemarie Hendrikz. Annemarie and Anne Schuster have encouraged and sustained me along the way. Clive Kirkwood and the other helpful and knowledgeable librarians at UCT Libraries have provided access to a great deal of material and a wonderful space to work.

Russell Martin of Jacana Media has had to exercise special patience and painstaking editing, without which I might well have given up the task of distilling such a mass of information. I can only offer my thanks and praise.

My husband Geoff and all my family have provided help, support and encouragement along the entire way.

Index

155

9 780821 422786